th Weed,
he shelf
with it so
d it.

Hajo Riesenbeck and Jesko Perrey
Power Brands

1807 – 2007 Knowledge for Generations

Each generation has its unique needs and aspirations. When Charles Wiley first opened his small printing shop in lower Manhattan in 1807, it was a generation of boundless potential searching for an identity. And we were there, helping to define a new American literary tradition. Over half a century later, in the midst of the Second Industrial Revolution, it was a generation focused on building the future. Once again, we were there, supplying the critical scientific, technical, and engineering knowledge that helped frame the world. Throughout the 20th Century, and into the new millennium, nations began to reach out beyond their own borders and a new international community was born. Wiley was there, expanding its operations around the world to enable a global exchange of ideas, opinions, and know-how.

For 200 years, Wiley has been an integral part of each generation s journey, enabling the flow of information and understanding necessary to meet their needs and fulfill their aspirations. Today, bold new technologies are changing the way we live and learn. Wiley will be there, providing you the must-have knowledge you need to imagine new worlds, new possibilities, and new opportunities.

Generations come and go, but you can always count on Wiley to provide you the knowledge you need, when and where you need it!

William J. Pesce
President and Chief Executive Officer

Peter Booth Wiley
Chairman of the Board

Hajo Riesenbeck and Jesko Perrey

Power Brands

Measuring, Making and
Managing Brand Success

WILEY-VCH Verlag GmbH & Co. KGaA

All books published by Wiley-VCH are carefully produced. Nevertheless, authors, editors, and publisher do not warrant the information contained in these books, including this book, to be free of errors. Readers are advised to keep in mind that statements, data, illustrations, procedural details or other items may inadvertently be inaccurate.

Library of Congress Card No.:
applied for

British Library Cataloguing-in-Publication Data
A catalogue record for this book is available from the British Library.

Bibliographic information published by the Deutsche Nationalbibliothek
Die Deutsche Nationalbibliothek lists this publication in the Deutsche Nationalbibliografie; detailed bibliographic data are available in the Internet at <http://dnb.d-nb.de>.

© 2007 WILEY-VCH Verlag GmbH & Co. KGaA, Weinheim

Printed in the Federal Republic of Germany

Printed on acid-free paper

Typesetting   Kühn & Weyh, Freiburg
Printing and Binding   Ebner & Spiegel GmbH, Ulm
Cover Design   init GmbH, Bielefeld

ISBN: 978-3-527-50282-0

Table of Contents

Why you should read this book

Brands. Is there any other topic in modern management about which so much has been published in recent years? The authors range from university professors to practitioners, advertising »gurus«, and consultants. On paper, their collected works would weigh many tons, leaving the impression that all aspects of branding have been covered in rich detail. Why then a new book from McKinsey on brands?

The initial idea emerged in response to the concerns of many managers about the shortcomings of existing concepts and tools. At the one extreme, many texts are so theoretical that companies can't use them without major adaptations. At the other extreme, you find easy-to-read popular points of view on the world of branding that everyone can agree with, but which also fail to offer practical tools or guidance. In dealing with these concerns in the many projects we have conducted in the area of branding, we saw our competence increasing and, with it, our confidence about being able to cover the topic in a practical, realistic, and detailed way. Many McKinsey teams have developed effective instruments in their marketing projects, which we know help our clients to better understand the complex issues of branding and how to manage their brands more effectively. Some concepts and tools evolved through intense cooperation with universities over some years–in particular, the concept of brand relevance, developed in cooperation with Professors Meffert and Backhaus of the University of Münster and with our McKinsey alumnus Dr. Marc Fischer of the University of Kiel.

These concepts and tools have proven successful in many projects in completely different industries. The results motivated us to pull together McKinsey's diverse know-how on individual aspects of successful brand management into a holistic approach that top management could quickly grasp and apply. We also knew from discussions with our own McKinsey editorial review board and external parties that brand management was a hot topic on the top management agenda. The total amount of money potentially spent ineffectively and inefficiently is just too large to leave decisions on branding to lower-level specialists or third parties.

Brands are an increasingly important issue not only for top management, but also in top management's discussions with analysts. For many acquisitions, for example, the questions often revolve around how to handle the acquired brands. Which ones have high value? Which ones can be given up? And what potential for value creation can be extracted from the acquired brands? Some companies excel at exploiting the potential of the brands they acquire, as BMW has shown with the Mini. Others simply kill acquired brands or let them fade away over time. We believe that these decisions should not be based on gut feeling or left up to luck. Instead, top management should have a fact-based, quantitative way to make brand decisions and to explain them to their stakeholders.

We saw this as a challenge, an ideal one for McKinsey. Our traditional strengths could be exploited: careful attention to detail, fact-based approach, analysis-driven recommendations, and systematic follow-up and control of impact. The challenge of applying this approach to brand management, where a belief in gut feeling and luck still largely prevails, beckoned irresistibly and drew us into what proved to be a highly motivating and satisfying journey.

When you take a closer look, you realize that marketing, unlike other management functions, really lacks great unifying breakthroughs. Marketing science has developed more and more into a niche field, where scholars talk to one another in their journals, while marketing practitioners have trouble understanding their theories or have simply stopped listening. Brand managers, on the other hand, along with ad agencies and the media, have followed their own course. The media have all developed their own specific quantitative metrics. Brand managers can define their own market research so that the results will prove their hypotheses. Under these circumstances, it is no surprise that senior management's trust in marketing decisions has declined, reducing any willingness to spend increasing amounts on brands. Faced with increasing pressure for business performance and transparency, boards and investors expect clear plans and quantified results.

To meet expectations and regain credibility, marketing and brand management need to demonstrate much greater professionalism, that is they need to take a more systematic and more quantitative approach to brand management. Power brands are just pure luck? That won't fly today. Brand success can be managed. This book will show you how. Our holistic approach, McKinsey BrandMatics®, provides senior executives with a complete framework for evaluating brand performance better, and gives marketing and brand managers a rich tool kit, illustrated with many examples, for managing brands more effectively. McKinsey BrandMatics® will help you make better brand decisions on the basis of data and facts and thus equip you to systematically manage your company's brand success.

In our experience, many common (and sometimes very obvious) mistakes can be prevented by rigorously applying BrandMatics®. Equally important, it provides practical guidance on allocating resources to better exploit brand potential–a critical source of internal growth. In tough times, simply cutting costs again is seldom enough. Nor is acquiring a company an automatic recipe for success: companies manage to integrate an acquisition and capture the theoretical growth potential in only about half the attempts made. Thus the challenge remains: get more growth from the existing business. Your company's brands are the trump cards in your hand.

When we published the first edition of this book for the German market in February 2004, our ambition was to get the ball rolling on systematic brand management in German-speaking countries. The examples and illustrations we chose were therefore very well known in those markets. We were thrilled by the book's success and many positive reactions from readers. After adding to and improving our concepts, we published the second German edition in August 2005. By then, many global clients were asking us for an English version. We therefore proceeded to adapt our book to global markets. In doing so, we have tried to choose brand examples known or readily understood around the world. *Power Brands* has German roots, but we are convinced that it will be useful in your home market as well. We know from many international projects that, as different as individual country markets may be, a unified global approach to the art, science, and craft of branding is the only way to manage the complexities of global brands successfully in a rapidly changing world.

Acknowledgements

The many positive reactions to the first two editions of *Power Brands* in German (entitled *Mega-Macht-Marke*) encouraged us to publish a version more accessible to an international readership. For the English edition, we have updated and internationalized many examples, added new steps, and described advances in our thinking and further ranges of application.

Many people participated in the writing of this book. Our thanks goes first to our advisors outside of McKinsey, Professors Klaus Backhaus and Heribert Meffert of the University of Münster, who not only contributed to the rich exchange of ideas between scholarship and practice, but also participated actively in the development of some individual concepts and instruments. We also thank our alumnus Dr. Marc Fischer of the Department of Innovation, New Media, and Marketing at the University of Kiel for his research and analysis and for his suggestions on the chapters about brand relevance. Furthermore, a special thanks goes to Professor Henrik Sattler of the University of Hamburg for his support in advising and coordinating the international market research on brand relevance.

We are also grateful to all of the companies that granted us permission to reproduce their proprietary graphics and texts, such as Audi, Beiersdorf, Deutsche Post World Net, Henkel, Katjes, Linde, Orange, Samsung, Skoda, Sony Ericsson, and Volkswagen, and also for their cooperation regarding case examples and other contributions. Our very special thanks, too, to Chris Burggraeve at Coca-Cola and Prof. Dr.-Ing. Wolfgang Reitzle at Linde for their stimulating and informative answers in our interviews, and to Dee Dutta at Sony Ericsson Mobile Communications, who shared his systematic and structured approach to allocating and evaluating marketing spend. We also very much appreciate the case example from the French telecommunications market contributed by Jean Baptiste Coumau, managing partner of Izsak Grapin & Associés and member of the Blue Ocean Network, and Emmanuel Josserand, professor at the University of Geneva and associate researcher at CREPA University of Paris Dauphine.

Many colleagues at McKinsey helped make *Power Brands* possible: Jürgen Schröder, our partner colleague in Düsseldorf, contributed materially to the development of many of the tools we discuss, very often in collaboration with the University of Münster. Thomas Barta, Nicole Baumüller, Jens Echterling, Christoph Erbenich, Harald Fanderl, Tjark Freundt, Fabian Hieronimus, Ansgar Hölscher, and Patrick Metzler supplied valuable insights and examples from their consulting practice. Our expert researchers, Saule Serikova and Geoffrey Sherburn, devoted countless hours to researching and verifying individual brands and brand stories, with support from their colleagues in McKinsey Research & Information Services.

We also owe a special debt of gratitude to our colleagues Thomas Meyer, our European Branding Practice manager, and to Mathias Kullmann for their great support in coordinating this project and in updating, internationalizing, and expanding the book. A very special thank you also to Ivan Hutnik, our editor, for his incisive questions, practical suggestions, and expert editing of our drafts. As for the first two editions, publishing coordination was again in the capable hands of Hella Reese, Rainer Mörike, and Daniel Münch. With their unstinting dedication and expert support, our assistants, Ms. Michaela Dülks and Ms. Denise Kranepoth, also once again helped us to advance steadily towards completion of the manuscript.

This third edition would never have come to be without the thoughtful and detailed comments we received on our very first drafts. We sincerely thank Winfried Wilhelm and Dr. Axel Born, both members of our Editorial Review Board, as well as Prof. Heribert Meffert for their valuable critical examination and suggestions regarding the original manuscript of the first German edition. Very warm thanks for their support of this first international edition go to our partner colleagues in McKinsey's European Marketing Practice, Johanna Waterous and Yoram Gutgeld, and especially to Trond Riiber Knudsen, who has been advocating an international edition of *Power Brands* for a long time.

Finally, our thanks go to Jens Kreibaum and his colleagues at our publishers, Wiley–VCH, for their enthusiastic and experienced support.

We wish our readers interesting discoveries, rewarding insights, and every possible success in implementing BrandMatics® and hope that sharing our experience will contribute to the creation and development of new power brands.

Düsseldorf   *Hajo Riesenbeck*
November 2006   *Jesko Perrey*

1.
What Brands Can Do,
and What Makes Them Strong

What has led six companies to have already paid EUR 100 million each just to secure their place as a sponsor for the 2010 FIFA World Cup in South Africa? Why does Procter & Gamble spend over EUR 6 billion in advertising each year? What it is that made companies spend USD 369 billion on advertising during 2004? Why is it that consumers are prepared to pay much more for a Mercedes or a BMW than for a comparable vehicle from Kia or Hyundai? And why are some people willing to pay enormous sums for a Rolex watch or a Louis Vuitton bag?

The answer is simple: brands. Brands, as these examples show, are the true giants of the modern world of consumption, dominating the household budgets of consumers and the investment calculations of companies. They not only shape millions of purchase decisions and countless company decisions, setting prices and determining profits; they also influence our perception and behavior, our self-esteem, our estimation of others, and our value judgments.[1] Put simply: brands shape people and markets alike.

1.1 What brands mean for consumers and companies

Brands are omnipresent. They address us directly in public, and subtly in the most intimate spheres of our lives. They stimulate our desires and form the hubs in the network of goods that typifies advanced consumer societies. No one can escape their influence. They are the emblems of a global economy, advancing well ahead of the financial markets and visible from much farther away than the turrets of the company's headquarters. »Brand-holder value« is the increasingly esteemed partner of »shareholder value.«

The message is clear: there is hardly a bank or an insurance company, a company in the automotive or telecommunications sector, a machine tools manufacturer, or a chemicals, electricity, or gas supplier that now ignores the growing importance of brands. Even public institutions such as the armed forces, state pension providers, and the EU have sat up and taken notice.

Brands shape our perception and our behavior

Perception is reality. It can also determine success or failure. Largely sub-consciously, we pigeonhole people according to the car they drive, the clothes they wear, and the accessories they surround themselves with.

Picture a smart, modern building made of glass, the offices of a company. The foyer is decorated minimally with designer furniture, clear lines, quality materials. A well-dressed receptionist guides visitors from the foyer to a conference room equipped with the very latest high-tech equipment, from the lighting system to the projector. Clearly an ultra-modern, profitable company with a young and dynamic staff. Wrong! In fact, it is an old, established transport company whose managing director has a weakness for modern architecture and the latest technology. But our first reaction is to believe what we see.

We use brands as lifebuoys in the flood of signals and information we are presented with. Take the launch event for a new BMW model: Ralf Schumacher, with his brother Michael, holds forth on the technical details; Coca-Cola, Red Bull, and Beck's provide the refreshments; Jennifer Lopez and Robbie Williams sing their latest hits; and reporters from *Time, GQ, Paris Match,* and *Hello magazine* take endless photos for their forthcoming editions. Who could resist such a brand? Who would turn down the invitation? Now take another event, this time launching a new vehicle produced by an Eastern European manufacturer. The catering consists of local store brands, the winner of a pop competition provides the entertainment, and a local paper covers the event. Brands save us time in that we do not have to check, challenge, classify, and critically weigh up everything before we make a decision to act. They are »an established, unmistakable mental representation of a product or service in the mind of the potential consumer.«[2] This representation is formed at all the points where we come into contact with the brand, including the product itself, advertisements, and word-of-mouth (see fig. 1.1).

Brands can mark class boundaries–or blur them. For some, owning a Rolex, a BMW, or a Louis Vuitton bag helps demonstrate, to themselves and to others, their membership in a particular social stratum. For others, brands can be used as a way of breaking free from their class shackles. Maybe they starved themselves to be able to afford that BMW, but once in it they drove into a different milieu.

The otherwise luxury-loving wine expert also blurs class boundaries when he serves his guests champagne from the discounter Aldi. Choosing to shop at Aldi, maybe even making a point of it, is not so very different

Fig. 1.1: A holistic concept for brand management: Experience the brand at all customer touch points

Choice of banks	Brand drivers	Customer touchpoints (examples)	Interactions (examples)
?	■ Reliable ■ Fast ■ Simple ■ Friendly	Cash service	■ Availability ■ Ease of use ■ Telephone support ■ ...
		Customer service	■ Competence ■ Friendliness ■ Ability to access full data ■ ...
		Direct service	
		Statements	■ Clarity ■ ...

Brand perception is a reflection of customers' individual experience of the brand at all points of contact

Source: McKinsey

from buying a luxury item. »Cheap« can itself be a strong and even a chic brand.

This bipolarization effect can be seen across industries; consumers are both trading up (and prepared to pay premiums for products they emotionally relate to) as well as at the same time trading down (and looking for savings for products that they don't feel passionate about) (see fig. 1.2). As a result, companies that find themselves stuck in the middle are facing increasing challenges and are showing much lower growth rates than both the premium and the »no-frills« providers.

Of course, private label brands are not to the liking of producers of traditional brands, and not just those of champagne. Consumer spending on private label personal care products is rising quickly, having increased globally from USD 4.3 billion in 2000 to USD 7.4 billion in 2005. Procter & Gamble is taking this private label threat very seriously. In May 2006, it filed its largest-ever trademark infringement lawsuits against a raft of private label copies, involving nine of their brands such as Head & Shoulders shampoo, Old Spice aftershave, and Crest toothpaste. It is clear that the world's largest consumer goods company is prepared to respond aggressively to the threat.

What Brands Can Do, and What Makes Them Strong

Fig. 1.2: Polarization effect

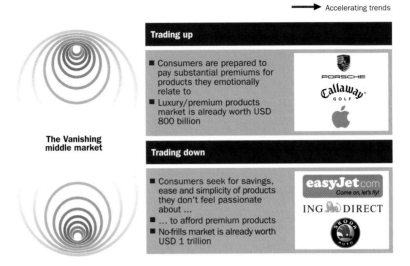

Source: Trading Up, Harvard Business Review, McKinsey

National brand associations are also responding to the threat of private label brands. For example in mid-2003, the German Brands Association (*Deutscher Markenverband*) launched a EUR 25 million poster and print media campaign with the slogan »The brand. I wouldn't buy anything else« taking on its challengers from the discounters' camp. Similarly in 2005, the Hungarian brand association ran a EUR 1.23 million campaign with the slogan »You can trust a true brand blindfolded« in an attempt to further strengthen brand awareness among consumers who were already loyal to brands to some degree. (see fig. 1.3).

Despite the power of brands, more and more frequently consumers are buying something else. Many previously anonymous or bland private labels (also sometimes known as »own brands« or »house brands«) have long been offering rather more than just »me-too« products, and they are doing well with their innovations in the competition for customer favor. More and more supermarket private label brands are giving themselves a distinctive profile by investing large amounts in publicity and up-trading. Consumer researchers predict that within a few years supermarket private label brands will gain a 50-percent share in the food retail market. The brands associations have woken up to this evil, as they see it, and are no longer mincing their words. For example, the 2005 campaign run by the Austrian Associa-

Fig. 1.3: Campaigns by brand associations

Brand-name merchandise:
I won't put anything else in my shopping bag

Good brands contain everything that is good for your child

Source: German Brand Association, 2003

Don't pinch pennies on refreshments

Look for the brand-name product!

Source: Austrian Association of the Branded Article Industry, 2005

tion of the Branded Article Industry (*Österreichischer Verband der Markenartikelindustrie*) treats the competition with own-brand labels literally as »a battle between good and evil.«

No product group is safe from encroachment by private labels. Even the safest, most established areas, where the newcomers were long powerless, are now reporting a dent in sales due to competition from private labels. Take tobacco products, for example, where private label brands have made little headway in Europe overall. The German market is the major exception. Here, while private label brands accounted for only 7.5 billion cigarettes in 1997, just five years later sales had topped 22 billion, an increase of nearly three times. In the two years following this, 2003 and 2004, sales fell dramatically across the market following increases in tobacco tax. But the losses were differentiated: sales of branded cigarettes fell by 22 percent, while sales of own-brand cigarettes dropped by just 14 percent.[3]

Have brands, then, lost their former power? Are the days when they dominated the market long gone? Not at all; in fact what is happening is that new species are developing on the brand landscape, leading to greater biological diversity. Old, established or: well-established branded articles

What Brands Can
Do, and What
Makes Them
Strong

must gather their strength as never before if they want to hold their ground or even gain new territory.

Brands both need and fear publicity. In today's information society, our beliefs, thoughts, and behavior are more and more subject to external stimuli. Companies that do not communicate well across all channels, or that fail to publicize their company and brand profile, soon stop being noticed by consumers and ultimately disappear from the market. What is more, the media act as an independent force and can praise a company or a brand to the skies one day and write it off the next. Their actions cannot be steered by the companies themselves. Napster, for example, went from being a well-known music download brand to one that currently achieves only moderate financial success. The Napster brand, although it initially received widespread attention in the media, was severely damaged by the negative publicity it received following attempts by music copyright holders to sue the company (and individual customers) over breach of copyright. Even after these problems were sorted out, Napster was unable to recover fully, its share price having dropped from USD 25 to USD 3. It has now been overtaken by competing online music-download sites.

Though communication is vital, this doesn't necessarily equate to advertising spend. The Spanish fashion chain Zara operates in a world where marketing spend generally amounts to 3 to 4 percent of sales revenue[4], but it manages to do without any advertising at all. In the 62 countries where the brand is now present, the company to date has not spent a single cent on marketing campaigns. Zara's sole means of advertising is its highly styled stores, always located on the best city streets and designed by a sizeable team of top window designers. Potential customers see the goods in the store windows as they walk through the city and hear the store recommended by satisfied customers—and no more is needed to sell fashionable items of clothing by the million. It works beautifully: Zara's sales revenues have grown on average 17 percent per year (faster than its arch-rival H&M). In 2005 they opened 129 new stores around the world.[5]

Companies and their brands: A special relationship

Brands can immunize. While a media push is often very helpful for a company, negative publicity can be very dangerous. Nevertheless, companies that have continually built and promoted their brands in a well-founded and fully rounded way can survive media attacks relatively intact. Thus a top brand like Coca-Cola can shake off an incident, such as the scandal over contaminated cans in Belgium in the summer of 1999, within a few weeks and without much further ado.

Less strong brands have a harder time of it. Coke's bottled water brand Dasani, which was launched in the UK in January 2004, was an initial success until a newspaper article in March disclosed that in fact it was simply treated tap water. This was then followed two weeks later by the UK authorities finding that there were concentrations of bromate in the water, a carcinogenic substance if taken in excessive quantities. This second blow to the brand was enough for Dasani to be recalled from the UK market. Likewise, the pasta manufacturer Birkel threatened to disappear from the market altogether after a relatively minor product contamination case, despite the fact that the national media did not give protracted coverage to the event.

Brands live and survive. The best product names can also survive attacks of quite a different kind to the media coverage mentioned above. Entire companies can go under, yet their brands are not sucked into the depths after them. Maybach, the luxury car brand from the 1920s and a symbol of German quality engineering, all but disappeared in the Second World War. However, the brand was so strong that it lived on and was revived by the Daimler-Chrysler group in 2000. Even without advertising, brands do not simply disappear. They can survive the drought like plants in a desert, waiting for the warm rain of fresh investments to flower once again in abundance.

Strong brands are like living organisms. The lifecycle theory, which predicts that brands generally die off after passing through phases of boom and then saturation, has been shown to be wrong. Strong brands such as Nestlé (since 1867), Heinz (1869), Coca-Cola (1886), Johnson & Johnson (1887), General Electric (1892), Maggi (1897), Mercedes (1902), Osram (1906), and Nivea (1911) have reached a legendary age and yet remain forever young. Market and brand leaders like McDonald's, Marlboro, and Nokia are just as much on everyone's lips today as Apple, IBM, or Microsoft. Classic brands such as Harley Davidson and the Mini or Sinalco can be revived and even attain new heights.

It is the brands that truly claim this longevity, not the companies themselves. After fifty or a hundred years, who can remember the firms' founders, its managing directors, the first board, or its core production plants or headquarters? But everyone knows the brands (see fig. 1.4).

Brands generate strong impressions and powerful feelings. When consumers hear the name Marlboro or just see the red Marlboro box, they immediately associate it with freedom and adventure, the cowboy riding across the plains. Nike evokes similarly strong, if quite different associations, with its

Fig. 1.4: Some strong brands

What Brands Can
Do, and What
Makes Them
Strong

Fig. 1.5: Brand logos create distinctive mental representations

images of athletics, performance and lifestyle. The Lacoste crocodile immediately triggers thoughts of sporty luxury, or even the tennis court at Wimbledon, while McDonald's golden arches make many people's mouths water. And the Coca-Cola bottle with its red label and brown liquid makes many people suddenly feel thirsty (see fig. 1.5).[6]

Brands generate tangible value. Apart from creating strong impressions, brands also generate tangible value. They create price premiums, help to recruit the best talent, and save sales cost due to their »pull« on customers. Perhaps most important of all, companies with strong brands frequently outperform the stock market. Recent McKinsey analysis shows that the fifty stocks listed in both the *Business Week*/Interbrand Top 100 Brands and the S&P 500 index have outperformed their peers by 1.5 percent a year over the past ten years (see fig. 1.6).

Three factors determine the brand's perceived added value

As shown by many examples, three factors determine the promise of a brand as perceived by the consumer–and thus its value for a company (see fig. 1.7).

1. *Image benefit.* Brands help consumers express who they are, contribute to self-esteem, communicate this to others, and enable them to claim allegiance to particular ideas or social groups.

2. *Information efficiency.* Brands are information carriers. They say something about the provenance of the item, help with recognition, and provide us with orientation. They act as lifebuoys in the flood of signals and information.

What Brands Can
Do, and What
Makes Them
Strong

Fig. 1.6: The impact of brands

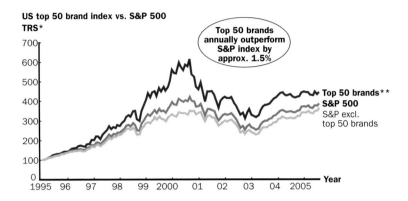

* Total return to shareholders
** 50 companies belonging to Interbrand top 100 brands 2005 as well as to the S&P 500
Source: Datastream, Interbrand 2005, McKinsey

3. *Risk reduction.* Brands lower the consumer's risk of making a wrong purchase decision. Branded products promise consistent quality and a lower
level of depreciation. Brands offer a safe choice, creating a basis of trust
between the manufacturer and the consumer and then providing continuity in this relationship.

The VW Golf brand (badged »Volkswagen Rabbit« in North America)
provides a good example of these three components of added value. For decades, the Golf brand has been a constant, almost universal presence on the
roads of Europe and North America. The Golf brand bundles together
everything that the consumer needs to know about the vehicle. Reliable
quality and solid construction combined with decent prices in the used-car
market limit the risk in buying a Golf. Embodying a sporty drive and a
youthful image, »the Golf generation« shows the Golf as an expression of
the driver's identity and membership in a particular social group. However,
the difficulties faced by the new Golf model in defending its position in the
market show that even strong brands can face challenges; the strengths of
the brand have not transferred automatically to the new model.

The Golf is typical of the current challenge. Today, even the strongest
brands must make headway in turbulent waters. Two trends can be
observed: on the one hand, worldwide the number of registered brands is
increasing dramatically. In 2005 there were nearly twice as many internationally registered trademarks worldwide as there were ten years before.

Fig. 1.7: Brands fulfill three basic functions

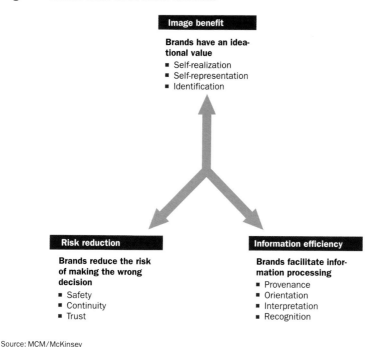

Image benefit

Brands have an ideational value
- Self-realization
- Self-representation
- Identification

Risk reduction

Brands reduce the risk of making the wrong decision
- Safety
- Continuity
- Trust

Information efficiency

Brands facilitate information processing
- Provenance
- Orientation
- Interpretation
- Recognition

Source: MCM/McKinsey

The dramatic expansion in the number of brands has inevitably given the consumer almost too much choice. In the past thirteen years the number of brands available in a typical grocery store has tripled, having risen from 15,000 to over 45,000. On the other hand, in consumer goods there is greater concentration, with fewer manufacturers and a greater focus on core brands. Unilever, for example, reduced its brand portfolio from some 1,600 brands in 2000 down to 400 core brands in 2005. So, despite the overall proliferation of brands, the leading companies are thinning out their brand portfolios and are focusing only on the brands that are strong enough to face tomorrow's challenges. For brands, it is quality that counts.

Tougher times require more effective brand management tools

In today's environment, where no investment is wasted, it makes little sense to allow an advertisement or a TV commercial, that an has been developed at significant cost simply to run its course and then disappear in a puff of smoke with no way of calculating its effectiveness. Advertising budgets need to demonstrate the highest possible impact. »Scattering losses« of 50 percent or more are by no means a law of nature. Rather, they are the result of insufficient analysis, shaky methodology, and dubious strategies.

It's no longer only the advertising gurus who dominate the scene with their creative but often imprecise gestures, however good that creativity might be. To complement the necessary creativity, they also need the expertise that can provide them with rational insights and analysis. Investing in brands is in many ways similar to other investments. Who would invest in a production facility, a research and development center, or a new head office without first examining the necessary commercial and financial groundwork to make a clear assessment of the probable payoff?

A shift toward a more professional approach to marketing and more efficient processes has been gaining pace recently. A literature search of the international journals reveals that more than 5,000 articles on branding have been published in the past five years alone.[7] Despite this flood of academic and practice-oriented publications, the right tools for effective and efficient brand management are still under debate. Experts are currently analyzing the basic factors underlying brand power, how best to describe them, and what their precise functions are for consumers. They are also looking into what makes brands strong, and what makes them weak.

While this debate continues, McKinsey has developed its own approach called BrandMatics®. This book uses this approach to reveal how companies can measure, make, and manage brands effectively without throwing creativity overboard.

1.2 The Secret of Strong Brands

What makes a brand strong? What distinguishes Marlboro from Camel, Nokia from BenQ, and Mercedes from Kia? One answer that is commonly given to this question is that a brand becomes dominant and full of life when everyone in its target group has internalized it as »well known.« Though this might be a very common assumption about what makes a brand successful, it fails to distinguish the great brands from the also-rans.

Brand awareness, and the often corresponding high scores for brand recognition in market research evaluations, is not enough in itself to secure a place among the front-runners. Such indicators, however popular they are, actually say very little about consumers' buying preferences. Market share and profit margins are far more revealing when it comes to describing a brand's position. Companies that achieve a bond with buyers and produce customer loyalty that cannot be matched by the competition are the brand winners. The right strategy for brand management can be summed up in a single, simple sentence: strong brands need buyers–and repeat buyers.

Coca-Cola is a good example, Coca-Cola drinkers are particularly loyal to their brand. In Germany for example, 52 percent will only drink »their Coke.« By comparison, just 10 percent of Pepsi drinkers will drink only Pepsi-Cola.[8] This one fact is enough to indicate the relative strength of those two major cola brands in that market.

Three elements of success: The trinity of *art*, *science*, and *craft*

For management, the strongest indicators of brand success are market presence, profitability, and customer loyalty. Companies that want to ensure this sort of brand strength for the long-term need to achieve a harmonious blend of three elements underlying good brand management: *art, science, and craft.*

The *art* is in endowing the brand with a superior brand proposition, keeping it consistent yet up-to-date and executing it as creatively as possible. The *science* is measuring and understanding the brand's performance. The *craft* is managing the brand rigorously in all its individual aspects throughout the organization.

Naturally, brands do not have to attain perfection in all three areas in order to be strong. Inevitably, companies have different approaches in their areas of focus, as well as different strengths and weaknesses. Nonetheless, however well a company masters an individual element, this will be of little use to them if they do not also achieve a basic minimum standard in the other two elements as well (see fig. 1.8).

We will now look at each element in some depth. We will start with the art of the brand, as this is the most familiar and widely accepted aspect of brand management, before moving on to the science and the craft.

Art: Superior content generates emotions

First, brands must have the right content in order to appeal to customers and to generate demand. They need to move us emotionally so that we find them appealing. They need to appear trustworthy in their claims. Companies, faced with the challenge of choosing the right attribute from among a mass of similar-looking technical and non-technical features, hardly know

Fig. 1.8: Three elements underpin excellent brand management

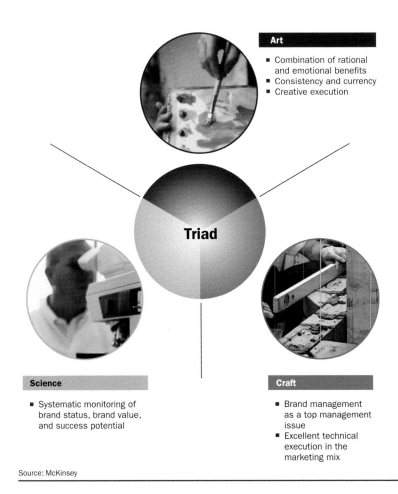

Art
- Combination of rational and emotional benefits
- Consistency and currency
- Creative execution

Triad

Science
- Systematic monitoring of brand status, brand value, and success potential

Craft
- Brand management as a top management issue
- Excellent technical execution in the marketing mix

Source: McKinsey

where to start. Should they focus on rational elements, for instance, in terms of delivery, or on the more emotional elements that they think will speak to customers' feelings?[9]

In fact, strong brands always do both, although the balance between the two varies. There are hardly any strong products or services that are not at least as good as the competition in their rational elements, and they are usually better in one or two attributes. At the same time, real brand champions, Marlboro, Nike, or Porsche, for example, show champion-like qualities in their emotional elements, too.

What Brands Can
Do, and What
Makes Them
Strong

Nivea is another good example. Every Nivea product features a rational product benefit and backs this claim up with research and information. This approach goes back to its introduction in 1911, when Nivea produced the first long-lasting oil-in-water emulsifier that wasn't based on animal and vegetable fats and so wouldn't go rancid. This scientific approach continues. The company's research center employs over 150 dermatological and cosmetics researchers, pharmacists and chemists. Today, according to the company, Nivea Visage DNAge products contain a »combination of cell-active Folic Acid and Creatine to protect the skin cells' DNA against future external damage«; their Anti Wrinkle & Firming Crème features a »unique patent-pending antioxidant complex, including Vitamin's A & E and sunscreen (SPF 4)«; while the Nivea for Men Revitalizing Lotion Q10 has a »combination of Vitamin E and SPF 15« to help protect against UV rays.

The rational product benefits are not just displayed on the packaging, they are also backed up by numerous product tests and, even more importantly, by the trust placed in them by large numbers of customers. At the same time, the brand is positioned in a clearly emotional way as a »gentle care« brand, supported by soft-focus photos and carefully chosen images that build a consistent identity, closely tied to central values of the blue »aura«, true values, and a code for genuine »close to touch« human togetherness. The product's appeal is thus aimed equally at customers' emotional and rational sides; this is what gives the brand its competitive advantage (see fig. 1.9).

This combination of emotional and rational elements is also part of the brand appeal of luxury goods, even though these are commonly perceived to be purely emotional. For Louis Vuitton products, for example, the customer's self-profiling plays a major role in the purchase and justifies the price difference compared with competitor products. At the same time, however, the materials used in the product are very high quality: the finest leather, tanned by hand (using plant extracts), and water- and scratch-resistant. It is this combination of quality (rational) and prestige (emotional) that is fundamental to the brand's strength.

Audi is another example of a brand that successfully blends emotional and rational elements. The brand's positive image is due, to no small extent, to its progressive design, its quality, and its advanced technology. The quality claim »*Vorsprung durch Technik*« (»Advanced engineering«) was introduced internationally on the back of the legendary Audi Quattro, with its permanent all-wheel drive and its success in the World Rally Championship at the beginning of the 1980s. The TDI concept developed by Audi engineers in 1989 was revolutionary and widely acclaimed. Building on

Fig. 1.9: Nivea: Appealing simultaneously to both emotions and reason

Germany 2004   United Kingdom 2005   Spain 2006

Source: Beiersdorf AG

this reputation, Audi launched the new FSI series-production engine in 2002, following from successful trials in motor sports. The brand further backed up its claim to leadership in the area of design with the introduction of the immensely successful TT model in 1999. Audi is not just proclaiming technological excellence but is also selling technological sex appeal (see fig. 1.10).

At the same time, emotional positioning alone will not make a brand strong if rational benefits are missing. C&A faced this problem in the early 1990s with its TV and cinema commercials (including its »Daydream« campaign). The commercials appealed greatly to the young target groups and even won industry awards, but the reality in the stores was different. Large rummage tables with cheap T-shirts and other bargains conflicted with the emotional world depicted in the commercials in terms of décor and product presentation. Potential customers were so disappointed that they seem to have avoided the shops for a long time afterwards. C&A managed to resolve this problem at the end of the 1990s. It did so by refocusing on the brand's traditional core positioning and values. This change in focus in its campaigns has seen C&A become increasingly successful in attracting its target group of families with below-average to average incomes back into its stores. As a result, the company is managing to hold its ground.[10]

What Brands Can
Do, and What
Makes Them
Strong

Fig. 1.10: Audi: Advanced engineering

1986   2005

Advanced engineering

Source: Audi AG

For consumers, emotional advertising without a rational basis is like a vacation brochure whose attractive pictures do not match up to the reality. This is ultimately a form of advertising that can have a negative impact.

Samsung: Making the journey from mass-market producer to premium brand

It requires a great deal of patience to transform a cheap brand into a premium-sector brand, but growing competition from China and else-where means that many companies have little alternative. Until well into the 1990s, the Korean electronics manufacturer Samsung earned its way by producing cheap products and by acting as a third-party manufacturer for premium brands such as Sony.[11]

The transformation from mass-market producer to quality brand man-ufacturer began at the end of the 1990s. This was prompted by the Asian financial crisis, which led to staff reductions of around a third and the realization that, as an increasingly high-wage country, Korea would soon no longer be able to compete with China in the mass-market segment. As a first step, the management established a global marketing function, thus underlining the importance of marketing for a company that had previously been dominated by an engineering mentality. Next, Samsung supported the development of the brand by bundling marketing activities across the company, stopping the production of cheap products in many countries and concentrating instead on innovative digital products with exclusive designs. While its competitors were still clinging on to cathode ray tube technology for television sets, for instance, Samsung made the strategic move into new digital technologies such as LCDs and plasma screens. This helped it break with its image as a cheap product manufacturer and move into the category of premium manufacturer. At the same time, the company tried to strengthen the emotional promise of the products and raise the brand's profile. As part of this strategy, Samsung became a leading sponsor of major sporting events, such as the soccer World Cup and the Olympic Games, as well as paying EUR 73 million to have its name emblazoned on the chests of the London soccer club Chelsea.[12]

Today, the results of this transformation are evident. The company's claim to be a leader in technology is reflected at the product level with the first mobile telephone featuring television, mobile phones with integrated high-resolution digital cameras with up to 10 megapixels, the world's lightest 12-inch laptop computer, weighing in at just under a kilo, and the world's largest plasma screen at 102 inches. Samsung, with its current team of 470 designers, was beaten only by Apple at the 2004 IDEA awards for design. And Samsung is one of the world's fastest-growing brands, recently winning honors from Interbrand and their Best Brands Awards.[13]

Making headway in Europe is proving much tougher for Samsung than in many countries in Asia, South America, Eastern Europe, and even the United States. In Germany, for instance, though the trend is highly positive, with Samsung's sales up by more than 20 percent in 2004 and 2005, unprompted brand recognition is low, at just 30 percent in 2004–a long way behind market leaders Nokia and Sony. Samsung's brand image is »cool« and »driven by technology,« partly as a result of their marketing slogan »DigitAll. Everyone's invited.« Nonetheless, in a digital world, manufacturers can no longer hope to differentiate themselves by a technology focus alone.

The challenge for Samsung is to change how European consumers see the brand–their mental representation of it. Samsung's management has realized that they must strengthen the emotional elements of the brand in order to develop it further. In an interview with *BusinessWeek* in 2005, Samsung's Global Chief Marketing Officer Gregory Lee stated: »In the past, our communication was all about the product. There wasn't a real story to it. We are really trying to tell a story about how it fits into consumer lives in our newer communications.« [14] Therefore, in mid-2005 the company launched a new advertising campaign »Imagine,« hoping to use this to change the brand's positioning with a jump into the premium sector. They are also now drawing on the full range of brand communication options: alongside traditional TV and print advertising, Samsung is increasingly using promotions, events, sponsoring, on-line advertising, and PR. Established brands such as Sony, Philips, and Nokia are watching closely.

Art: Modern creativity and consistency are no contradiction

Strong brands are consistent, preserving and maintaining their brand names. They do not make constant changes to their positioning, their target group, or their image. At the same time, strong brands innovate constantly, building on the brand promise.

At first sight, being both consistent and innovative might appear something of a conundrum. Nivea provides a good example of how a brand can be both highly innovative while always remaining consistent with its brand values. Nivea Crème's distinctive packaging, a blue container with the Nivea name spelt out in prominent white script, is a vital part of this. Today's packaging has a long pedigree and can be traced right back to 1924, when the distinctive blue container was first introduced. Just as important is that Nivea's brand promise from its introduction has been that of providing high quality and gentle skin care at a reasonable price, using a straight-forward approach. It is this reputation for dependability and trustworthiness that has stood the company in good stead throughout the decades. At the same time, Nivea has innovated constantly. As far back as 1930s, Nivea introduced sun cream into its product range. Since then there have been regular product innovations, with a large expansion in products from the 1980s onwards. Today Nivea's products include specific care products for different skin types, shampoos designed for various hair types, and products for men as well as women. All these innovative products are distinguished not only by their packaging but also by Nivea's brand values of gentle care. Nivea's consistent innovation and brand promise are well recognized in the industry, and Nivea has won many international prizes for its products, including the 2005 Natural Beauty Award for its Nivea Visage Q10 Advanced Wrinkle Reducer Eye Crème.

BMW's well-known and successful brand vision »the ultimate driving machine« has been at the heart of the brand's promise since the 1950s and has made a large contribution to BMW's global success.

As well as being consistent, BMW has also always strived to be innovative. This aspect of the brand is well captured in a speech made by BMW's chairman, Helmut Panke, at the Paris Motor Show in 2002: »The BMW brand stands for a promise of fascinating, individual automobiles and we shall continue to keep our promise in this respect. A part of this promise is never to build a boring BMW.« This is a promise that BMW has lived up to since its beginning. In 1923 BMW made their first major innovation in the automotive sector when they designed and built a motorcycle that used a driveshaft rather than a chain to drive the rear wheel. In 1961 BMW launched the 1500, a powerful compact sedan with front disc brakes and four-wheel independent suspension. This innovative specification cemented BMW's reputation for fast sports cars. In 1988, BMW was the first motorbike manufacturer to introduce ABS. In 2000 BMW's radical redesign of its vehicles' styling ensured that they would catch the eye and remain modern. This combination of a consistent message and constant innovation has led to global success for the company. In the United States, for instance, sales have increased at a compound annual growth rate (CAGR) of 14 percent since 1991.

Another example of the advantages of consistency is that of Coca-Cola. While Coca-Cola has always stuck to its classic curly logo and the color red, Pepsi has changed its logo nine times since the brand was created. Perhaps the most radical change was that made in 1998. With a budget of USD 500 million, Pepsi changed its colors from red, white, and blue to just blue. The reason given by the company for the redesign was that the old logo was not distinctive enough and that it was imperative that Pepsi distinguish itself from Coca-Cola. [15] In 2003 the next update occurred, aimed at stressing the brand's youthful image. Yet in the vast majority of markets, these continuous makeovers have neither helped it catch up with Coca-Cola nor ensured it a better brand image. [16]

Marlboro has shown nearly the same persistence as Coca-Cola. Since Marlboro's makeover by Leo Burnett in the 1950s, it has never questioned its positioning as a cigarette brand associated with freedom and adventure. The image of the cowboy (since 1963) and the Marlboro red (since the 1950s) have remained constant over a very long period, while the contents of the advertising campaigns have been adjusted many times in line with current fashions and new innovations in cigarettes have been used to refresh the brand. The umbrella brand name Marlboro was only extended with the launch of Marlboro Lights in 1986. In 1994 Marlboro Medium was introduced, and today there are additional product extensions such as Marlboro Menthol, Marlboro 100, and Marlboro Blend 29 (see fig. 1.11).[17]

What Brands Can Do, and What Makes Them Strong

Fig. 1.11: The cowboy is constant, the camel wanders

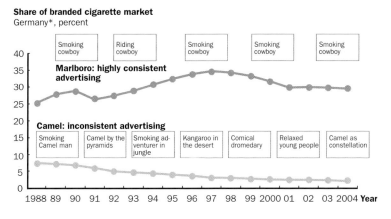

Share of branded cigarette market
Germany*, percent

* West Germany only up to 1990, all of Germany from 1991
Source: *Deutsche Tabakzeitung*

Outside the United States, where there has been somewhat greater consistency, Camel, the number two brand, has changed its positioning constantly over the same period. In Germany, for example, it has moved from the Camel man as an adventurer with a hole in his shoe in the 1970s and 1980s to the leather-clad toy camel in the 1990s, to the image of the relaxed young professional between 2001 and 2004, and finally back to the camel. The image of the brand has been altered so many times that it has become almost devoid of meaning. Today, while Marlboro controls 19 percent of the European market, Camel has a share of slightly less than 5 percent.[18]

In the market for coffee in Germany, the Tchibo brand has remained consistent over decades. The product was originally presented by portly, soberly dressed »Tchibo coffee experts« who spoke knowledgeably about the product. Direct advertising came later but the brand's essence remained unaltered. In a shrinking market that was increasingly shaped by strong own-brand labels, Tchibo managed to lose only 2.5 percent market share between 1992 and 2004 (from 17 percent in 1992 down to 14.5 percent in 2004).[19] In contrast, the competitor product Jacobs Coffee, Germany's best-selling branded coffee, lost 11.5 percent market share over the same period (from 30 percent down to 18.5 percent). This dramatic deterioration in the Jacobs Coffee brand has been caused by its constant, sometimes dramatic changes in positioning. An earlier campaign, which played on the bad consciences of conservative, family-oriented housewives, was replaced

What Brands Can
Do, and What
Makes Them
Strong

with campaigns aimed at single households. Jacobs lost its original target group but was unable to win over the new one. That resulted in the brand being discounted and sold at a very low margin in stores. This lack of consistency led Jacobs into a vicious cycle from which the brand is only now starting to recover.

Similar examples to those of Marlboro versus Camel or Tchibo versus Jacobs can be found in almost every sector, from mobile telephones to beer.

Art: Creativity doesn't necessarily mean winning prizes

In addition to ensuring that it has superior content and keeping the brand up-to-date (while consistent), a very important aspect of the art of brand management is the creativity of its communication. In this context, the advertising industry has always been seen as of central importance to brand management, but in a society flooded by multimedia, many believe that advertising is no longer as effective as it once was. Consumers are becoming more and more like overfed fish that swim on regardless, indifferent to the thousands of pieces of advertising bait placed before them every day. As a result, many companies are questioning the service offered them by advertisers and greater fiscal discipline is being brought into marketing, moving it into line with other functions in terms of measuring P&L. The demand is that advertising must be seen to deliver results.

Still, some brands do manage to achieve consistent competitive advantage by means of better creativity in their communication; they know exactly where to place the bait so that the fish will bite. Strong brands are highly effective in the way in which they use creative campaigns to distinguish themselves from the competition, to strengthen their brand image, and thus ultimately also to generate correspondingly high sales. Examining the advertising used by brands over many years reveals a number of particularly successful long-lasting examples: for example, Lucky Strike's purist approach limited to the packaging and a witty headline, Red Bull's unique scribbles, and Sixt's smart and often provocative advertising motifs.

Leading brands demand great advertising. In the best creative partnerships, the demands of a great brand will push the advertising agency to the peak of its creative capabilities, producing a positive synergy that infuses the entire sector with energy. For instance, there can be no doubt that it is the automotive sector that sets the standards for advertising in Germany, where automotive campaigns dominate creativity competitions.[20] In the highly regarded German Art Directors Club (ADC) competition, for instance, the Golf GTI (branded »Volkswagen GTI« in North America) and Mercedes G-Class campaigns took the two top places in 2005, while BMW came in fourth. Campaigns for German automotive brands have also received international recognition. For example, the Mercedes CLK convertible commercial, »The Sound of Summer,« produced by Springer & Jacoby in Hamburg, won a Golden Lion at Cannes in 2005; it successfully recreated the feelings associated with a warm summer's day when driving a Mercedes on a lonely country road.

Often, really successful creative advertising contains something that might be irritating, provocative, or funny, whether in pictures or in words; the campaigns of Lucky Strike, Sixt, and Red Bull are again all good examples of this. Many other major brands take a less confrontational approach, however, and are no less successful for it. For brands such as Nivea, Beck's, and Marlboro, creativity is primarily about constantly renewing a consistent brand in as simple and catchy a way as possible, occasionally introducing new elements to revitalize the message. This ensures that the brand remains up-to-date over the years, and although it may appear less original to the judges of creativity contests, it usually brings better dividends. Dr. Rolf Kunisch, until May 2005 CEO of Beiersdorf AG, the company behind Nivea and other brands, acknowledged at the October 2003 German Marketing Conference that this approach had a very positive impact on their bottom line.

There is, of course, no one-to-one correlation between prizes for creativity and commercial success. The Camel campaigns have been creative but this is not sufficient in itself; almost every prize for advertising creativity was accompanied by bad news about the brand's market share. The C&A campaign during the mid-1990s was so creative that music from the ads even made it into the top charts. Nonetheless, customers were not pulled into its stores in large numbers.[21] The limitations of advertising are well recognized. Marketing specialists believe that no brand campaign has a greater than 50 percent likelihood of actually influencing sales positively.[22]

As a result, the advertising industry has stopped focusing exclusively on creativity, although prizes remain as important as ever. To be eligible for the Global Effie awards, for instance, a campaign must have run in four or more countries in two or more regions of the world. Mary Lee Keane, executive director of the Effie Awards says, »Effie winners share the honor of finding the perfect combination of strategy, creativity, and media to resonate with consumers.«

Ogilvy & Mather Chicago's campaign for Unilever's Dove brand, »Campaign for Real Beauty« won the top prize in 2006. Ty Montague, chair of the 2006 Grand Effie Judging Panel commented, »The Dove campaign was the clear Grand Effie winner. It is a successful campaign rooted in a powerful human and cultural insight: that beauty has heretofore been defined by the media and is actually defined much differently by real women.« Not only did the campaign succeed in showing that the brand had a strong point of view on beauty, but it also succeeded in growing the brand's value share across its key European markets by 13.5 percent. Silver Global Effies were awarded to DDB Worldwide for the McDonald's »I'm lovin' it« campaign and to Fallon for the Citigroup »Live Richly« campaign. A Bronze Global Effie was awarded to EURO RSCG for its Peugeot »407–Let's talk« campaign.

Science: The challenge of accurate measurement

The second element of good brand management is *science*. Tracking a brand's status by carefully and systematically analyzing its strengths and weaknesses means much more than simply measuring brand awareness and advertising recall. Brand analysis requires effective tools. Although many major brands have long had at their disposal instruments tailored for tracking their brand, the majority of marketing managers and agencies still measure their brands' strengths and weaknesses using a limited range of indicators. In today's world this is no longer sufficient.

Advertising tracking instruments used to confirm the value of the advertising investment tend to focus solely on the level of awareness and recall. This can all too easily lead to the conclusion that if the brand enjoys a high level of awareness and recall, then the investment is well spent and the brand is strong. In many cases, this is not the case. This problem can be seen in teaser campaigns, for instance. Here, companies have wasted millions of euros on advertising which aimed to attract attention to a brand before it actually appeared on the market. Take Daewoo, for example. In 1995 the Korean car manufacturer spent approximately EUR 15 million on an awareness-building campaign in Germany using a variety of media channels. The campaign showed a mouth shaped into the form of a kiss, which supposedly explained how the brand name is meant to be pronounced. Though the campaign did have some effect on increasing brand awareness and advertising recall, it had no impact at all on sales. Three years later, Daewoo's market share was just 0.5 percent. Unfortunately, this tale doesn't have a happy end either. In 1998, following a major financial crisis, the company sold off its automotive business to a group of international investors (a leading member of which is GM of the United States).

The experience of E.ON was similar. Arising out of the merger of Veba and Viag in June 2000, E.ON needed to establish itself both as a corporate brand and as a product brand for electricity. The company ran extensive teaser campaigns and later featured product endorsements from Arnold Schwarzenegger and Veronika Ferres. The »Mix it, baby« teaser campaign ran across Germany on billboards, in newspaper advertisements, and in TV commercials. Originally it featured just a red background; two weeks later, the brand name E.ON appeared. However, the advertisements made no reference to electricity or to power. As a result, the brand became well known, but consumers associated it with a wide range of different products and very rarely with what the company actually provided. From a corporate branding point of view, the E.ON campaign was successful. E.ON certainly was able to strengthen awareness of its corporate brand among corporate stakeholders, for example, the capital markets. From a product marketing perspective, however, the success of the advertising in financial terms was, not unsurprisingly, modest.

The E.ON »Mix it, baby« campaign initially won great plaudits for its creativity. But in terms of product marketing and branding, it did not produce the desired results. Only just over a thousand customers switched to E.ON as a result of the campaign, which cost the company an estimated EUR 22.5 million for product advertising alone (resulting in an acquisition cost of around EUR 20,500 for each new customer).[23] Given an average annual revenue of approximately EUR 600 per customer, this campaign could never pay for itself, even if customers remain loyal to E.ON for the rest of their lives. Yet the E.ON brand was considered strong because it achieved a high level of brand awareness within a short time; just four months after its launch, market research showed aided brand awareness of 93 percent and unaided advertising recall of 66 percent. Fifty percent of Germans knew the »On« slogan, and 85 percent knew it came from E.ON.[24] The problems wasn't recall, the problem was revenues. Both the company and the agency appear to have had a very inadequate understanding of how the advertising would translate into income.

Strong brands generate strong sales and profits. They need buyers, repeat buyers, and a price that ensures they will continue developing and bringing in revenue. Accordingly, the tool used for measuring the brand needs to be one that is able to dissect brand performance in terms of its impact on the bottom line and not just its effect on consumer consciousness.

The German power sector appears to have learned from E.ON's failed trial; in 2004 the sector invested approximately EUR 50 million in traditional advertising, just over a third the level of five years earlier. German energy providers are only now regaining confidence when it comes to brand communication, although with placing a greater emphasis on connecting the advertising to the product and to specific target customer segments.

What Brands Can
Do, and What
Makes Them
Strong

At a time when products and services are becoming increasingly inter-changeable, many companies and advertising agencies are nonetheless con-tinuing to go down the road of focusing their campaigns solely on raising brand awareness. In today's environment this is unlikely to yield the desired results. This is shown by the campaign of Pets.com. In 2001, the dotcom pet store reached high levels of awareness by using a sock puppet that became a popular phenomenon. The puppet starred in ten commer-cials, including a well-appreciated 2000 Super Bowl ad, and was even the center of focus in a float entered in the Macy's Thanksgiving Day Parade. Despite the character's popularity and all the public interest that was cre-ated, Pets.com was out of business nine months later.

The lesson that needs to be learned is that such success does not come without a price, in that only a few consumers actually remember the con-tents or even the product being advertised. This is the key area where many current measurements of brand strength fail to deliver; the company remains in the dark as to whether the consumer is clear about the product benefits and, if they are clear, how then these benefits connect to consumer purchasing behavior. Rather than pursuing awareness and recall, what is needed is analysis that takes the more difficult road of identifying how the advertising campaign promotes the emotional and rational benefits of the brand itself.

Naturally enough, measuring brand strength will always take brand awareness as its starting point. But high awareness is only the start for a strong brand; though prerequisite for success, high brand awareness is not enough in itself to make a brand truly strong. For this to happen, consu-mers must also be familiar with the contents of the brand in terms of the product or service offer, and the target group must be willing to give greater consideration to the brand than to its competitors when making purchase decisions. In other words, the brand must perform well along the entire purchase funnel.

This is not to say that a strong brand performs equally well at each stage of the purchase funnel. It is rare that a brand outperforms the competition at every stage, from initial awareness right up to brand loyalty; most brands reveal slight weaknesses at one stage or another. Nevertheless, for strong brands these weaknesses are rarely severe.

Accurate measurement of a brand's relative strengths and weakness in the brand purchase funnel is the starting point for making further improve-ments to the brand. Nivea is an example of a brand that has strengths throughout the funnel. Nivea is today one of the leading cosmetics brand in Europe and a world leader in skin care, as well as in many other personal hygiene segments, such as baby care, sun care, and deodorants. Brand awareness for Nivea Crème is very high; in Germany, 85 percent are aware of the brand, 48 percent say they like it and, most importantly, 39 percent use it regularly.[25] This strength along the brand funnel has seen Nivea's global sales increase by five times since 1990, reaching EUR 2.8 billion in 2005.[26] At each stage, Nivea's brand managers measure the brand's success in the funnel, dissecting every aspect of the indicators, reinforcing positive trends and taking immediate action to target even the slightest negative change.

Good brand managers look below the surface at their brand's strengths and weaknesses. They make detailed measurements using objective standards and constantly hone their measurement techniques. Companies such as P&G, Henkel, and Unilever spend several million euros each year on market research, and the heads of their market research departments are some of the best-known experts in the field; top management listens to them before making decisions. Henkel, for example, was one of the first companies in Germany to define clear measurement categories and to write performance into its contracts with advertising agencies. In 1990 the company introduced a bonus system for its washing detergent advertising, extending this to cosmetics in 1995 and to other segments later on.[27]

Craft: Brand management is CEO business

Ultimately, brands can only survive if their management is first class. Such excellence requires continuity and a steady hand. This usually means the leadership of one person who has the depth of experience to ensure that the brand core remains unchanged over years (better still, decades) while being kept up-to-date through innovation and advertising. This is a natural role for the CEO; the more senior the manager, the more likely that the brand management will be successful. One of the best examples of how to do this well comes from Porsche. Wendelin Wiedeking, CEO of Porsche since 1992, believes that brand management is a key part of his job: »A company's brand is like its crown jewels, and it requires equal care. You don't keep hauling them out and you don't wear them on every occasion, but you have to remember that they are there and need careful cleaning and looking after.«[28]

These are words that many an advertising agency would do well to listen to. Too much tinkering is more likely to damage the brand than enhance it. Deciding what will add to the brand's strength and what will not is a top management decision. The Smart car did not fit the Mercedes-Benz image, so it was better to choose a new brand name. Nivea can offer shampoo and maybe nail polish besides its creams and care products, but it should not offer a household detergent. The core of the Porsche brand will always be in its sports cars, even if certain sports cars, such as the Cayenne, may succeed in breaking down category barriers.

The CEO or other chief caretaker of a brand must have internalized the brand core in order to be able to manage the trade-off between generating additional revenue potential and weakening the brand. Brand management is a top-management issue–it should not be delegated to product managers, external agencies, or another third party.

Craft: Using the brand's strength to its greatest extent

Besides requiring an experienced guiding hand, *craft* also requires translating the power of the brand concept into a reality on the street. In other words: for brands, execution is all. Companies with strong brands ensure attention in every detail.

Take McDonald's, for example: the company unfailingly achieves the same quality in its products in every McDonald's restaurant and in every country in which it operates. It insists on perfection in every detail and on scrupulous adherence to fixed standards and documentation in each stage of the process, from selection, purchasing, and processing of raw materials, right up to the preparation of individual products. To ensure that all staff members are aware of these operating standards, McDonald's managers around the world are trained in special »Hamburger Universities« where they learn the basics as well as the latest developments.

McDonald's ensures that all raw materials and ingredients are subject constantly to almost obsessive visual, physical, chemical, microbiological, and nutritional checks. Suppliers, like the restaurants themselves, work according to the HACCP principle (Hazard Analysis and Critical Control Point), a risk analysis of production processes originally developed by NASA to protect astronauts from the risks of food poisoning.[29] All McDonald's products have sell-by times (not dates), after which they are disposed of. Fries must be sold within seven minutes of frying, and hamburgers can remain on the pre-warmed sales racks for a maximum of ten minutes. After this, the food is binned. Another factor in McDonald's success is the speed with which customers are served. McDonald's prescribes, down to the second, exactly how long different operations should take. A Big Mac bun, for example, is toasted for exactly 35 seconds and no longer.[30]

McDonald's beats other fast-food providers in the areas of product quality and speed. In other areas, such as restaurant décor, friendliness of service, and location, McDonald's does not have a decisive edge over the competition. It doesn't need to. McDonald's corroborates the statement made earlier: a strong brand needs only one or two outstanding attributes in its rational product benefits in order to hold its own against the competition. In its remaining attributes it doesn't need necessarily to be better, but neither should it have any significant disadvantages in the eyes of the target group.

Nokia also executes its brand strategy excellently. Jorma Ollila, former CEO of Nokia, says: »Why have we been a successful company? If you want a simple answer, it is getting the balance right between innovation and execution. In a technology business you need a tremendous amount of innovation, but with these volumes and growth, you need to execute or it will kill you. So, it is balance. I think we have done this better than anybody else.« [31] Nokia's success arises from the fact that it not only focused on getting its product and brand right, but its production and distribution right as well. Once it had done all these things, Nokia was in a position to almost double its global market share from 19 percent in 1997 to 35 percent in 2005.

The balance between all these elements is critical. The problems affecting Nokia in the first half of 2004 had their roots in this tension between innovation and execution. Probably due its very strong market leadership, the company had been focusing a little too much on exotic products while at the same time, quite unwittingly, giving scant attention to the trend towards clamshell phones. Once the error was understood, CEO Jorma Ollila took swift action to strengthen the company's customer insight functions and knowledge and, within a few months, demonstrated that Nokia was able to respond to customer needs (see fig. 1.12). In the first half of 2005, Nokia's market share strongly recovered [32] and, today, Nokia is once again the undisputed global leader in the cell phone market.

The Porsche 911 is one of the world's most successful car brands. Porsche has shown outstanding execution in the brand, positioning the product for that small segment of the market that values well-above-average acceleration, a sporty chassis, and strong design. Porsche has implemented this positioning in the 911's development from the design phase right up to vehicle testing. The concern for detail is particularly noticeable in the design. The typical Porsche Boxster engine should sound »powerful, somewhat metallic in places, unmistakable, but always pleasantly sonorous and restrained.« This sound is monitored by no less than fifty engineers in Porsche's acoustics and vibration technology section. They listen not only to the six-cylinder engine but to wipers, blinkers, door locks and light switches as well. The sound technicians check every moving part and correct even the slightest dud note. Every 911 has a distinct 911 sound.[33]

What Brands Can
Do, and What
Makes Them
Strong

Fig. 1.12: Nokia: A brand promising innovation

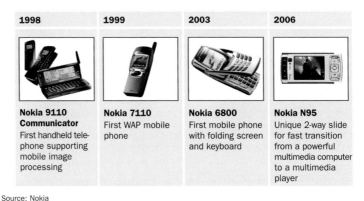

1998	1999	2003	2006
Nokia 9110 Communicator First handheld telephone supporting mobile image processing	**Nokia 7110** First WAP mobile phone	**Nokia 6800** First mobile phone with folding screen and keyboard	**Nokia N95** Unique 2-way slide for fast transition from a powerful multimedia computer to a multimedia player

Source: Nokia

Excellent execution is not necessarily limited to the product. Price, sales channel management, and details of communication can form key characteristics in strong brands. For the discounter Aldi, for example, price is the key; this is the competitive advantage that has made the brand strong. Right from the outset, Aldi stressed that every article they sold was cheaper than the equivalent elsewhere.

Aldi has turned simplicity of execution into a guiding principle, from its spartan stores to its narrow assortment of around 600 products. Logistics costs play a role in the renting of new branches: the stores must be accessible for articulated trucks and the aisles wide enough for maneuvering euro-pallets. Aldi's stores are usually located either on side streets near areas with a high frequency of passers-by or on the edge of town where there are good parking facilities and low rental costs. The comparatively narrow assortment of goods ensures simplicity in buying and handling, and the scale advantages give bargaining power in negotiations with suppliers. Aldi also keeps labor costs down by reducing management to an absolute minimum and having no strong central functions.[34]

The rapid rise of Lidl, Germany's second-largest discounter, is challenging Aldi in its market leadership. Lidl has copied many basic business processes from Aldi but offers a wider assortment of products, with some 1200 different items, including many more branded articles than its competitor. In response to this, recently Aldi has also started stocking branded articles like Mars, Bounty, and Kinder Country.[35]

One brand that has always been excellent in every aspect of execution is Coca-Cola. As early as 1923, the then-CEO Robert Woodruff made execution a key part of the brand by announcing that Coca-Cola should always be »within an arm's reach of desire.«[36] Coca-Cola has stuck to this motto, implementing it around the globe with a great attention to detail.

To realize this objective, Coca-Cola has systematically developed new sales channels: in addition to traditional food retailers, gasoline stations, and kiosks, it targets major sporting events and the like. Any remaining gaps in distribution are closed by means of vending machines; there are some one million of them in Japan alone, for example.[37] Coca-Cola continues to develop and perfect these machines, some of which feature the very latest technology, such as in allowing customers to pay by using their mobile phones.

Similarly, Coca-Cola's supply channel management is excellent: the product is always available at every sales channel. This is a critical competitive advantage for an impulse drink such as Coca-Cola, which needs to be available whenever the customer wants it. The product quality is also right, the packaging is constantly being improved, and the brand has an enormous emotional appeal. Such excellence does not allow for complacency, however. In 2004, Coca-Cola suffered a major setback in its German market when its market share dropped substantially as a result of its tardy response to new packaging regulations. At the end of the year, the company's share of the cola market had fallen to a little under 50 percent, compared with 60 percent in 2001.[38]

It is top management's job to ensure that day in, day out, the core elements of the brand retain their quality in every aspect. This is no easy task, of course, and things can go badly wrong as was demonstrated by the difficulties faced by the French holiday operator Club Méditerranée (Club Med). Today, Club Med is in decline, despite the consumers' perception of the brand still being very strong. After three years of shrinking income, Club Med's revenues for 2005 were just EUR 1.59 billion (following an average annual fall of 6.9 percent from October 2001 to 2004). While producing a significant loss of some EUR 94 million in 2003 and around EUR 44 million in 2004, the brand recovered slightly in 2005 to make a profit of EUR 4 million.[39] By then the brand was let down by many aspects of its operations, from the way the Club Med villages are decorated and furnished to the quality of the accommodation, the food, and the individual services on offer. With a new brand campaign in 2005/2006 and major reconfiguring of their villages management is yet again trying to win back customers.

The problems of Club Med are compounded by the fact that on the one hand it faces competition from fresher, younger businesses that are imitating its formula successfully (and without repeating its mistakes) while, on the other, its traditional clientele is migrating to other formats, such as low-cost holidays booked over the Internet. This doesn't mean that the club resort format no longer works, however. Robinson Club, for example, has shown that excellent execution produces a thriving business. Like Club Med, it provides holidays that are carefree, sporty, and active. Unlike Club Med, Robinson Club's market is not broad-based but oriented toward young, urban professionals. Today Club Robinson delivers this brand proposition in twenty-four resorts in nine different countries around the world. It ensures that it provides excellent quality in each Club Robinson resort in terms of accommodation, food, and sports facilities. The heart of its success stems from ensuring that every employee understands what is required to execute this brand proposition in all aspects of their service.

The secret of brand success: The brand trinity

Strong brands develop and prosper by achieving a harmonious trinity of *art, science,* and *craft*, whatever their particular focus. High-powered brands need powerful content–in both emotional and rational terms–and an image that remains consistent over many years without ever becoming outdated. Top brands maintain and develop their strength by tracking their status continuously according to qualitative criteria, such as their image, and quantitative indicators, such as market share and customer loyalty. Strong brands are also executed in a consistent and effective manner, as reflected in the marketing and through the actions of the entire organization, from CEO down to the shop-floor staff.

Only a few brands have been able to achieve this balance and maintain it over the longer term. Top brands do not usually excel in all three disciplines, as already mentioned. Instead, they tend to have one or two areas where they really shine, and they keep plowing away at the other areas.

For decades, Mercedes automobiles have stood for outstanding quality, reliability, and value retention. They immediately communicate the owner's membership in a certain status group. The design of the vehicles may not always have been avant-garde, and the sales teams may not always have been the most aggressive or obliging, but the organization's focus on building outstanding vehicles has ensured that the brand has remained competitive even through rough times. Yet even here it is not invulnerable, as recent discussions about the cars' quality and reliability have shown.

During the 1970s and 1980s, the Mercedes-Benz brand enjoyed such leadership in the luxury car market that it owned a practical monopoly in such areas as quality, safety, technological leadership, and exclusivity. One prominent example of the trendsetting innovation that formed the basis of its brand image was the very early introduction of safety components that are today almost taken for granted, such as airbags, seatbelt pre-tensioners, ABS (antilock braking system), and ESP (electronic stability program). Not without reason, Mercedes-Benz claims that it shaped the »future of the automobile.«

In light of this success, it may come as something of a surprise that until the late 1970s the company lacked a sophisticated marketing department or marketing representation at the board level. This has all changed, and today Mercedes' marketing is highly sophisticated and plays a much bigger role in the company, more so than at most other corporations. Mercedes-Benz brand management, which reports to the sales board, has been given the task of profiling the brand in such as way as to retain its character while reflecting regional peculiarities. For instance, at the start of the 1990s the company launched a new product and image offensive. The change in marketing style ushered in a new public image for the vehicle. Creative advertising campaigns gave the brand a younger image and brought its traditional values up to date, all the time leaving the brand core intact.[40]

Ikea, the largest furniture retailing chain in the world, provides another good example of how it is possible to produce harmony in the trinity of *art, science,* and *craft.* The Swedish furniture empire currently runs over 189 home furnishings stores in 23 different countries (237 stores in 35 countries as of August 2006 if one includes franchised stores) with revenues of EUR 17.7 billion in the financial year 2005-06. Around the globe, Ikea still stands for the concept launched by founder and owner Ingvar Kamprad in the 1950s: furniture and home accessories that combine function and quality at affordable prices (see fig. 1.13).

Ikea not only used creative and successful advertising campaigns to build itself into a strong brand but has also kept up a stream of convincing innovations, and not just in furniture. In 1996, for instance, Ikea set up a joint venture with the building company Skanska with the aim of building apartments and houses. For decades, Ikea had been providing furnishings for homes, so it seemed logical to start building the homes, too. BoKlok (Swedish for »smart living«), as the joint venture was called, set itself the task of developing living spaces that were of high quality and yet affordable.

The project's starting point was market research (the *science* factor). This research showed BoKlok that there was an attractive market in providing affordable homes to people on average or slightly less than average incomes. Its target group was primarily working people and young families

Fig. 1.13: Ikea: Expertly developed into a global brand

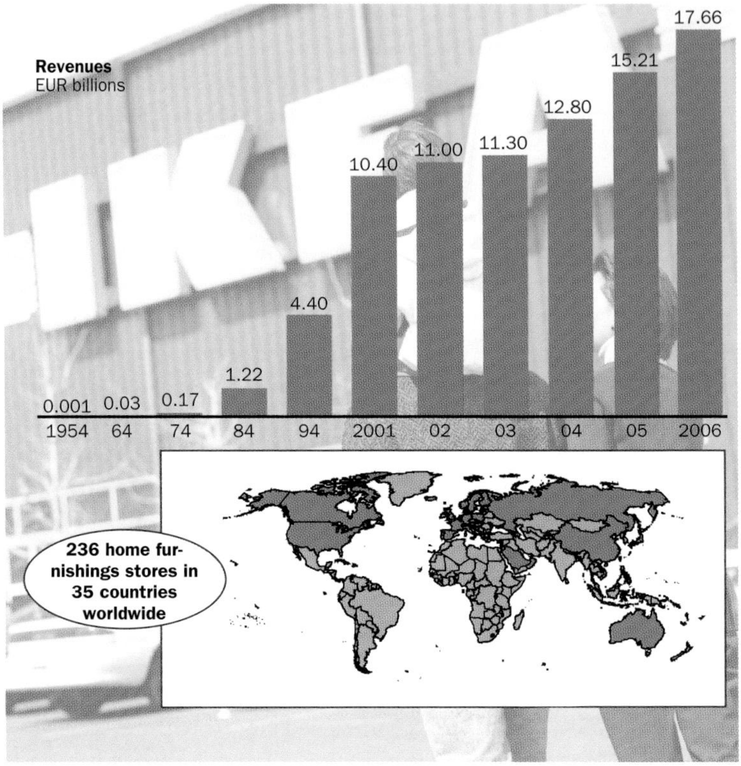

Source: Inter IKEA Systems B.V.

who had otherwise been priced out of the open market. What they were looking for was attractive and fashionable housing at an affordable price.

Exactly that is what BoKlok set out to create. In order to raise productivity and keep construction costs down, BoKlok took advantage of industrialized prefabrication for most sections of the building. The transport logistics were also developed by Ikea. The result is a two-storied house comprising six apartments that can be packed into twenty-five transportable »packages.« The design has created a flexible open-plan layout with high ceilings and large windows, giving the apartments a light, airy, and contemporary feel. Because of the high level of prefabrication, houses are ready to move into within six weeks; a project consisting of between three and six houses takes three to four months to build. The company Myresjöhus, once a subsidiary of the Skanska Group, is responsible for the building work, and the apartments are sold through the nearest Ikea store.

The apartments come with oak parquet flooring as standard in all living spaces, brightly painted walls in six different color combinations, a complete Ikea kitchen, and a washing machine. The gardens are available for communal use by tenants, who share responsibility for their upkeep. They have achieved their aim, as the apartments are popular and affordable. Since its inception, BoKlok has built over 2,000 units in Scandinavia. The average rent for a one- to three-room apartment made by BoKlok is EUR 350450. In 2003, it took the step of expanding into the UK and has been sufficiently successful there to be making plans now for further expansion to locations such as Ireland, France, the Netherlands, and the United States.[41]

Ikea shows consistency in the creative execution of its communication. Its most important tool for building relationships with its customers, apart from the stores themselves, is its catalog, some 174 million copies of which are printed worldwide in 48 different editions and 25 languages.

Since 1985, the company's campaigns have spotlighted ingenious solutions using Ikea products. A clear price message has also consistently formed a key part of this communications strategy. In the United States, Ikea's quirky »lamp« commercial has won major accolades at home and abroad, including the Grand Prix award in the film category for the world's best TV and cinema ads at the 50th Annual Cannes Lions. Using the tagline »Ikea unboring,« it communicates the lifestyle dimension of the brand in a funny and slightly satirical manner.

In Germany, Ikea has used a more emotional communication strategy, »Started living yet?« In 2002, the Hamburg-based advertising agency was given the task of selling home decoration as a lifestyle activity. The slogan they came up with has already become an advertising classic and won the agency a silver Effie in October 2004.[42] Today, Ikea is the best-known home furnishings brand in Germany, with current brand awareness at 87 percent. It has achieved this level by raising brand awareness by 10 percent in just four years. Other brand funnel measurements are similarly healthy; in terms of consumers' likelihood of making a purchase, Ikea leads with 47 percent saying they are likely to.[43]

Ikea's campaigns show that it has a lot more to offer than just decent-priced pine furniture and plastic chairs. Their message is that Ikea is a lifestyle brand and its products are attractive and stylish. As well as young people, Ikea is now targeting older, higher-income consumers and encouraging them to start shopping at Ikea, too.

Katjes: Brand management in a smaller company

The Katjes success story begins almost one hundred years ago. In 1910 Xaver Fassin brought home a recipe for making licorice with him from Sicily. His son, Klaus Fassin, used the recipe to make licorice in the shape of little black cats, calling the product *katjes*, the Dutch word for »little kitty.« His idea was so successful that in 1950 Klaus Fassin renamed his confectionery company, located in Emmerich on the German-Netherlands border, in honor of the product.

In 1996, Tobias Bachmüller joined the company as CEO. He put in place several measures to help the company achieve new growth. First he introduced a cost-reduction program, cutting back on administrative costs and pruning down the broad product portfolio. The money saved was invested in brand building and communication. »For branded companies, advertising is essential–even for small and medium-sized companies,« says Tobias Bachmüller, adding that products that are advertised run less risk of being delisted by retailers. Nonetheless, small and medium-sized companies in particular often question the value of investing in brands. Products and equipment can be seen and touched, brands cannot.

To make sure no advertising spend is wasted, Katjes decided to focus on the product with the highest sales, largest margin, and clearest differentiation from the competition. Yoghurt-Gums, a fruit gum made with real yoghurt, and the brand promise that it contains fewer calories than many other candies therefore became the focus of Katjes' public image. Since 2001, this image has been backed up by TV commercials featuring the well-known and much-loved supermodel Heidi Klum, which have pushed up (boosted) sales of Yoghurt-Gums considerably. Using celebrities in advertising generally gets a commercial or advertisement noticed from among the throngs of others. Creativity also plays a major role. For Tobias Bachmüller, however, having a consistent brand message is critical. For Yoghurt-Gums, the words »fat free« emblazoned on the packet and the slim figure of Heidi Klum are a perfect combination to appeal to the main target group, that of the figure-conscious, calorie-counting women aged between 20 and 40.

Katjes continuously monitors the impact of its advertising spend so it can optimize it for effectiveness and efficiency. Impact evaluations are available within two to three weeks and are used by the company to shape how it spends its advertising budget. Tobias Bachmüller stresses the value of having facts as a basis for management in helping build bridges by putting everyone in the company on the same page.

To help the company move into additional growth segments, Katjes has decided to change how it defines itself: no longer will it be a »fruit goods and licorice manufacturer« but a »confectionery manufacturer.« According to market research, this was how customers perceived the Katjes brand in any case. The change opened the company to making acquisitions in such areas as hard candy, fizzy powder (sherbet), and other categories. In its acquisitions strategy, Katjes concentrated on confectionery brands whose sales and marketing were underdeveloped. After acquiring relatively well-known German brands such as Dr. Hillers (peppermint candies) and Gletscher-Eis, Katjes bought Ahoj-Brause after it went bankrupt in 2002.

Ahoj-Brause is a fizzy powder brand that has been around for over seventy years but which had not been advertised for the past fifty. Katjes turned the brand around in a carbon copy of what it had done with its own brand: it pruned back the assortment, concentrating on the packets of fizzy powder; defined a brand message (»*Mach was Prickelndes*« or »Do something fizzy«); and launched TV advertising with a fitting celebrity, in this case Hape Kerkeling. The brand has been a major success. In 2003 sales of the fizzy powder rose by 45 percent, and it now makes up around 15 percent of Katjes' total business.

Building on such successes, the company has managed to more than double its overall sales in the past eight years to EUR 189 million. Katjes now has a strong presence in more than a dozen countries, which, along with its near neighbors, include Australia and much of Eastern Europe. Effective branding has helped Katjes establish its place in the highly competitive confectionery market.[44]

Strong brands can survive occasional mistakes

Trying to maintain consistency of a brand at the same time as keeping it up to date is a tall order, and managers sometimes make mistakes. But consumers forgive strong brands for such mistakes if they are corrected quickly and in full. A classic example is that of New Coke in the 1980s. In the attempt to counter falling market shares and consumers' preference for Pepsi-Cola in taste tests, Coca-Cola's management decided, in what was in retrospect surely a moment of madness, to change the recipe of Coca-Cola, a closely guarded secret that had remained unaltered for ninety-nine years. After extensive testing, the company believed they had come up with a mixture that people would prefer to both Pepsi and traditional Coca-Cola. The results of consumer acceptance tests looking into the psychological aspects of a new Coke were also positive. Thus in April 1985 the company decided to break all taboos and launch New Coke, spending a suitable amount on advertising, of course.

To say that New Coke was something of a disappointment is probably a masterpiece of understatement. The financial writer Stuart Crainer described it as »the marketing mistake of the century.«[45] The disaster took its course, accompanied by a storm of protests from customers. »It's as if God had dyed the grass pink,« complained fans of Coca-Cola. The company had to deal with up to 8,000 complaint calls each day and was bombarded with tens of thousands of letters of protest. Coca-Cola was taken by surprise by this massive rejection of its product but soon took appropriate remedial steps: it admitted to making a mistake and asked its customers for forgiveness. Within three months, in July 1985, the old Coca-Cola was reintroduced under the name Classic Coke and enjoyed a massive comeback. New Coke was still supplied to retailers, but its market share plummeted until it was finally dropped by the company. The big surprise for many was that the New Coke affair did not inflict any serious damage to the company's sales: between 1984 and 1985 sales rose by 7 percent. Coca-Cola had inadvertently proved that no brand is stronger.

It is not only Coca-Cola that can survive shooting itself in the foot. Mercedes-Benz shows how a strong brand can overcome even the most spectacular PR disaster. In November 1997 the company had assembled journalists from the Swedish automobile bimonthly journal *Teknikens Varld* to watch its brand new A-class compact perform the 50-meter slalom-shaped »Avoidance Manoeuvre Test,« commonly known as the »elk test.« At 60 kilometers an hour, watched by TV cameras and with journalists aboard, the A-class teetered on two wheels and then turned over. One of the journalists was injured. Soon the TV footage was being broadcast around the world, and the A-class had been labelled unstable and unsafe. New deliveries of the A-Class were suspended until February while engineers considered the situation. In just nineteen days, Mercedes had announced a plan and a timetable by which to set the problem aright. The introduction of an »electronic stability program« (ESP) cost Mercedes a little more than EUR 80 million. Within two months, the number of positive articles about the A-class's stability had overtaken the negative. For any lesser brand, failing the elk test so spectacularly would have inflicted severe, long-term damage. For

What Brands Can
Do, and What
Makes Them
Strong

Mercedes, there was no lasting damage to its reputation for producing well-engineered cars.

Companies also make mistakes with business-to-business brands, but even here the strong brands survive. In 1994, a calculation flaw came to light in the Intel Pentium chip, which according to Intel advertising was the best on the market. Thomas Nicely, a professor of mathematics at Lynchburg College, Virginia, had noticed that his new PC fitted with an Intel Pentium processor made rounding errors from the fifth digit onwards, even when making simple divisions. He complained to Intel straight away, but the company's reaction was dismissive. It said that it saw no grounds to take action, since the rounding error would be a problem for only a few specialists and thus not significant for the average user.

That this position wasn't sustainable should have been immediately evident to Intel. Intel's response provoked Professor Nicely to vent his anger publicly on the World-Wide Web at the end of October 1994. This led to over 10,000 further responses, all of which expressed outrage at the calculation flaw on Intel Pentium processor. The problem was discussed in more than twenty chat-rooms, and soon a parody of Intel's co-branding slogan was making the rounds: »Intel inside. Can't divide.« The stakes rose and soon news media from the world was reporting on the plight of the dumb chip.

Somewhat surprisingly, Intel was still unwilling to listen. Andy Grove, CEO of the computer chip giant, even went so far as to demand that customers prove that they were carrying out such advanced mathematical calculations before he would replace the faulty chips. This led to practically full-scale mutiny against Intel.

The problem escalated still further when in early December 1994 the computer giant IBM, then one of Intel's major clients, announced that it would replace all personal computers fitted with Intel Pentium processors and that from now on no computer would leave IBM's production sites with the faulty chip fitted. The stock markets were not slow to react; within minutes Intel's stock fell dramatically, reaching the point where trading was temporarily suspended. To top it all, the *New York Times* awarded Intel a Consumer Deception Award. After having made a mountain out of a molehill, a few days before Christmas 1994, Intel finally reacted. Three board members publicly apologized to customers and offered to replace all processors free of charge without asking questions and without users having to prove anything.[46]

The most surprising thing was that following these events, Intel's sales did not ultimately suffer: between 1993 and 1995 sales revenue almost doubled from USD 8.8 to 16.2 billion.[47] The lesson is clear: strong brands like Intel can even compensate for – temporary – poor management.

Strong brands that get the trinity of *art*, *science*, and *craft* right have such power over customers that, in extreme cases, they can even function successfully without any research and development, production, logistics, or sales of their own. Branded companies such as Red Bull, Adidas, and Porsche can ignore certain parts of the value chain altogether, outsourcing certain steps to third parties without damaging perception of the brand.

Red Bull, for example, has concentrated from the very beginning on the concept of the drink and its communication. The company does not own a single bottling plant, warehouse, or delivery truck. The fruit juice company Rauch, based in Rankweil in western Austria, takes care of worldwide production, and forwarding agents transport the product to the various national distribution companies. [48]

Similarly, the Adidas brand is so strong that consumers aren't worried about how the shoes are produced. This enabled Adidas to switch its production strategy in order to copy that of its major competitor Nike, which since its creation in 1962 has never owned its own production facilities and has had all its goods produced in Asia. »We don't need production expertise,« said Herbert Hainer, who took over as CEO of the then Adidas Salomon Group in 2001.[49] True to his word, by spring 2005 just 4 production units remained out of the 900-plus that had formerly belonged to the Group.

It is undoubtedly the case that brands such as these are highly valuable assets, but for those struggling on the periphery the question remains: How does one develop a strong brand? The remaining chapters set out the right approach to brand management, analyze what makes a strong brand strong, lay out the tools that managers will require for a full understanding, and look at the ingredients for success in developing a strong brand.

1.3 McKinsey BrandMatics®

Mastering brand management

More myths surround the process of creating and developing a brand than any other area of business management. This is because the art of a brand flatters the consumer, appeals to the emotions, and develops a resonance that it is hard to quantify. Indeed, the wit, originality, and imaginativeness of successful brands, such as Red Bull, Apple, and Nike show the importance of the intuitive and the creative. Strong brands have the ability to create their own myths.

Nonetheless, despite the undoubted importance of art, strong brands are seldom developed by art alone but by a careful mix of art, science, and craft; the role of science and craft in this mix often being underestimated. Take Red Bull, for example, a brand with strong appeal to the younger generation. Science played a vital role in developing a detailed understanding of the brand's market appeal to target groups; craft was central too, in ensuring outstanding execution and consistency in the management of the brand.

The story of Red Bull is illustrative of how art, science, and craft combine. Dietrich Mateschitz, the founder of Red Bull and former marketing manager of Blendax (later acquired by P&G), spent five years realizing his idea for launching a sweet, caffeinated beverage. His idea was to introduce a pick-me-up of the type he had come to know and appreciate during his travels in Asia. The brand concept was carefully planned. He developed every process in detail, from packaging to communication. Mateschitz then ensured the precise coordination of all the processes before launching and distributing the beverage in its first market, Austria, in 1987.

He was equally meticulous in introducing the drink in each subsequent market. Each national market was divided into »cells,« in which the goal was to make consumers aware of the new product within three to six months. The initial customer base was sought out and developed by specially trained teams that focused on locations where the young congregate, such as universities or clubs and bars. Once a loyal customer base had been developed in this manner, wide-scale distribution followed, typically two to three months later, using all the normal distribution channels, with a slight preference for restaurants over food retail. Only then did classic advertising begin, focusing primarily on television and radio.

The focal point of the Red Bull communication was and remains the product itself, with its clear positioning: stimulation of the mind and body. The design and color scheme of the drink cans reflect the product's positioning and demonstrate the meticulousness of the brand's planning. Some 100 different draft designs were commissioned before the final ones were chosen.

The intention of the final design is carefully thought out. The bull embodies strength, courage, and stamina. Cold colors, blue and silver, were used to represent the intellect, while hot ones, red and gold, were used to symbolize emotion. On the Red Bull Energy Drink, the logo is rounded out by the claim, »vitalizes the body and mind.« This claim was reinforced with the slogan »Red Bull gives you wiiings!« This catchy motto is designed to convey individuality, innovation, expertise, fun, and agility and thus promote the emotional values of the brand.

The Red Bull ads' creativity is kept direct, simple, and fun using cartoon sketches that through their humorous depiction of a bull have achieved a high degree of consumer recognition. New motifs and ideas for ads are developed within this formal consistency, ensuring that the product remains unmistakable for its market.

Red Bull has moved far away from traditional media in many aspects of its campaigns. Nowhere is this better exemplified than in its sports event Red Bull *Flugtag* (or »Flight Day«). These events are an innovative and creative form of marketing that supports the claim »Red Bull gives you wiiings.« Teams have to build and fly their own aircraft. What constitutes an aircraft is left to the imagination of the teams participating in the event. The teams are judged on three criteria: distance, creativity, and showmanship. The first Red Bull Flugtag took place in Vienna, Austria, in 1991. Since then, more than 35 events have been held around the world–from Ireland to San Francisco–attracting huge publicity and up to 300,000 spectators each time (see fig. 1.14).

Red Bull succeeded in achieving high brand recognition and market success through a well-measured combination of art, science, and craft. In contrast, there are numerous examples of brands that have placed an overemphasis on creative concepts, and that have neglected the aspects of science and craft.

There is no question that the creativity of advertising agencies is crucial in brand management–and will remain so for the foreseeable future. But their creativity needs to be applied in the context of the science and craft of brand management, and not independently of them. For many companies, accepting this simple fact requires stepping back from their current way of doing things and involves a complete readjustment of their brand management approach. It is senior management who must set this course.

Managing brands in the modern marketplace is very demanding. In-house departments often do not have the skills for the analytical side of this task and are sometimes overwhelmed by the demands placed upon them. As a result, instead of being presented with analytically well-founded concepts, management all too often gets nothing but a compilation of numbers that do not point to any kind of concrete recommendation. This lack of clarity means that even where the services of well-established market research institutes are used, their work does not capture the attention of senior management, however much it might deserve to do so. Nor are out-

What Brands Can
Do, and What
Makes Them
Strong

Fig. 1.14: Red Bull: Painstaking planning gave the brand wings

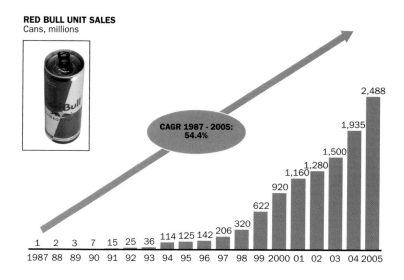

RED BULL UNIT SALES
Cans, millions

CAGR 1987 - 2005:
54.4%

1987	88	89	90	91	92	93	94	95	96	97	98	99	2000	01	02	03	04	2005
1	2	3	7	15	25	36	114	125	142	206	320	622	920	1,160	1,280	1,500	1,935	2,488

Source: Red Bull

side agencies and »marketing gurus« able to fill this gap. Not only does their core expertise lie in another field, but they are also not particularly interested in rendering their own work open to scrutiny through the use of objective measurement systems. All in all, management is not well served.

It is clear that management, in its desire to integrate the creative aspect of brand management with its other management processes, is turning increasingly today to academia and strategic management consultants. Until now, there has been little light even here. Instead, management is presented with a nearly incomprehensible jungle of concepts that all make the claim that they lay bare the economic value of the brand without producing the necessary transparency.

That this situation should prevail today is somewhat surprising. Whereas top management is used to receiving concrete business figures in terms of revenues, returns, capital ratios, costs, volumes, and productivity every Monday from virtually all areas of its business, branding has so far been the exception to the rule. This handicaps sound decision making and alienates top management from the management of one of the most vital compo-

What Brands Can
Do, and What
Makes Them
Strong

nents of success – the control of the brand. This is something we seek to redress here.

We believe that top management requires the integration of art, science, and craft for systematic, fact-based brand management. This requires creating a degree of transparency that has so far been lacking in the branding world. This transparency is essential if management boards are to base their brand management decisions on sound foundations.

The following chapters present a holistic approach to brand management. This includes systematic, qualitative indicators (e.g., brand image) and quantitative ones (e.g., revenue potential). We refer to this approach as BrandMatics®, as it provides a systematic framework for brand management. In the following pages, the individual tools and detailed concepts are organized into three topic areas: measuring, making, and managing power brands.

Measuring brands

When setting out to measure the brand, the starting point should always be a thorough survey of the current perception of the brand, from the point of view of both established customers and potential new customers.

The *brand relevance tachometer* provides answers to the often-neglected (but critical) question of whether and to what extent it is worthwhile to develop brands in a certain sector.

The *McKinsey brand diamond* is a framework for conducting a complete (image) analysis of all of a brand's emotional and rational factors to reveal what the brand represents to customers and non-customers.

The *brand purchase funnel* gauges the strength of the brand in comparison with competing brands, from the point of the initial awareness of the consumer to that of repeat product purchase by loyal customers. This analysis provides information for the refinement of the brand. It also helps to identify which brands in a brand portfolio will be the most effective in reaching a target group of customers.

Using the *brand potential approach*, brand managers can quantify the brand sales potential embedded in the purchase funnel and reallocate their brand investments in order to tap this potential.

Making brands

Taking the results of the brand diagnosis, the next step is to identify what actions need to be taken to build the brand.

First, the *analysis of brand drivers* helps identify those factors and customer needs that distinguish strong brands from weak ones in the purchase funnel. This defines the strategic direction and the initiatives that need to be taken to grow the brand. In most cases the fundamental *brand promise* will need to be adjusted (or even completely reformulated) to take account of the brand's current weaknesses. Of course, for this process to be effective in growing the brand, the brand promise needs to be anchored in the actual capabilities of the company's operating units (rather than those that the company might wish for).

The next step is to set up a *pathway analysis*. This translates abstract brand elements into practical and understandable terms, for instance, for the creative brief. Pathways analysis ensures that the brand is manageable within the company.

Brand portfolio management: While the professional management of a single brand requires the right mix of *art*, *craft*, and *science*, the task of managing an entire portfolio of brands is substantially more complex. However, with the support of some selected portfolio instruments, the BrandMatics® approach can also be used for systematic and successful brand portfolio management.

Many brands appeal to their customers in a primarily rational manner and thus appear relatively unattractive emotionally from a customer's point of view. To overcome this weakness, the *brand personality gameboard* provides an analytically grounded and almost playful tool for building or expanding the brand personality in a controlled and replicable manner. It takes the brand from its definition to communication and implementation.

Managing brands

Once the desired brand has been defined using the above-mentioned tools, the new or improved brand content will need to be put in place. This requires identifying the optimal budget and suitable media. This is the basic concept of *marketing return on investment (ROI)*.

The *brand cockpit* then ensures that the main criteria for brand success are continually measured and assessed. If the market environment changes or competitors react, the »instrumentation« of the brand cockpit allows the brand manager to initiate actions to manage the brand in a timely manner.

Even a brand with a well-defined brand promise and a sophisticated tracking system can fail, however, because it is not established consistently across all the relevant stakeholders within the organization. The *brand delivery concept* provides a systematic, three-step approach for creating a brand mindset in the organization, in translating the brand promise into concrete actions along all the customer touch points, and in ensuring its longer-term institutionalization.

Finally, in order for brand management to remain a top management priority, an appropriate *brand organization* is needed. The brand organization concept explores the range of alternative organizational structures that can develop effective and efficient processes to integrate all business units around the goals of brand management. These alternatives include, for instance, those that appoint a brand management board or that establish marketing and consumer intelligence departments that report directly to the CEO.

BrandMatics® is a holistic and consistent approach to brand management. That said, successful brand management is nearly always the result of strong partnerships. Often a key factor for success is the involvement of external service providers, that is, hiring a market research agency to conduct surveys or commissioning an advertising agency to design ways to communicate the brand proposition. The following chapters cover all these topics and reflect the experience of McKinsey's Marketing Practice regarding how senior management teams have used the tools and concepts of BrandMatics® to put brand decisions on a more objective footing, combining its qualitative brand features with precise and reliable economic data, and thereby minimizing the risk of making serious investment errors.

Notes

1 Kenning, Peter et al., »Die Entdeckung der kortikalen Entlastung,« in: *Neuro-ökonomische Forschungsberichte*, no. 1, 2002. University of Münster, Institute for Trade Management and Network Marketing, Prof. Dieter Ahlert. See also »Monetäre Markenbewertung: Die Marke als Kapitalanlage,« *Absatzwirtschaft* 2 (2004): pp. 26–41.

2 Meffert, Heribert, and Christoph Burmann, »Markenbildung und Markenstrategien,« in: *Handbuch Produktmanagement*, ed. Sönke Albers and Andreas Herrmann, (Wiesbaden: Gabler, 2000), pp. 167–187.

3 *Deutsche Tabakzeitung*, various years, 1997 to 2004.

4 Based on H&M (4 percent of sales volume), GAP (3 percent), C&A (4 per-

What Brands Can
Do, and What
Makes Them
Strong

cent). Cf. »Mode zum Anfassen,« *man-agermagazin* 1 (2004): p. 74; »Gestreifte Schals wärmen die GAP-Aktie,« *www.faz.net*, 28. Feb. 2003; »Zu modisch: C&A verlieren Kunden,« *Stuttgarter Nachrichten*, 7. June 2005, p. 10.

5 Annual reports of the Inditex Group and H&M Company, various years.

6 Cf. Fischer, Marc, Fabian Hieronimus, and Marcel Kreuz, »Markenrelevanz in der Unternehmensführung: Messung, Erklärung und empirische Befunde für B2C-Märkte,« in: *Arbeitspapier Nr. 1*, ed. Klaus Backhaus, Heribert Meffert, Jürgen Meffert, Jesko Perrey, Jürgen Schröder (McKinsey), Düsseldorf, 2002.

7 Results from a search performed by ABI/Inform of international academic publications.

8 Brand loyalty barometer from the 2001 Consumer Analysis by Bauer Media KG and Axel Springer Verlag AG, www.bauermedia.com.

9 Recent scientific research shows that the importance of rational vs. emotional brand aspects on the purchase decision varies across different industries and that it can be measured analytically. See, for example: Freundt, Tjark, Emotionalisierung von Marken, (Wiesbaden: DuV 2005).

10 »Bekleidungskette C&A zeigt Expansionsgelüste,« *Frankfurter Allgemeine Zeitung*, 7. June 2005, p. 20; Weber, Stefan, »C&A trotzt der Krise im Textilhandel,« *Süddeutsche Zeitung*, 3. June 2003, p. 22; Werner, Markus, »Werbung und Wirkung,« *Textilwirtschaft*, 20. Febr. 2003, p. 54.

11 »Das Comeback der Wow-Wows,« *brand eins Magazin* 3 (2005): pp. 44–50.

12 »Hippe Handys, träges Marketing,« *werben & verkaufen*, 13.Jan. 2005, pp. 22–24.

13 Ward, Andrew, »How Samsung Became a Global Champion,« in: *FT.com*, 5.9.2004.

14 »Samsung's Goal: Be Like BMW,« *BusinessWeek Online*, 1. August 2005, see http://www.businessweek.com/magazine/content/05_31/b3945107.htm

15 Roosdorp, Alexander, »Coca-Cola: Leistungspflege durch agile Marktkommunikation,« in: *Best Practice in Marketing*, ed. Tomczak, Torsten, and Sven Reinecke (Vienna: Wirtschaftsverlag Carl Ueberreuter, 1998), pp. 241–251.

16 »Corporate Identity – nur anders,« *Wirtschaftswoche*, 25. April 1996, p. 134.

17 Dingler, Rolf, »Der Prototyp für erfolgreiches Markenmanagement,« *FVW International* 22, 14.Oct. 1997, p. 112.

18 *Deutsche Tabakzeitung*, various years.

19 Tchibo brand only, excluding Eduscho Gala.

20 »Big Bang an der Côte,« *werben & verkaufen*, 30. June 2005, p. 34.

21 A number of campaigns appear to have been created solely for the purposes of the competition or copied from competitors to a large extent; cf. »Ärger mit Dubletten und Fakes,« *Horizont*, 24. March 2005, p. 23.

22 »Die Marke als Leuchtfeuer,« *werben & verkaufen*, 24. Oct. 2003, pp. 30–33.

23 »Vergiss es, Baby,« *Der Spiegel*, 18. Febr. 2002, p. 76.

24 Michael, Bernd M., »Wenn die Wertschöpfung weiter sinkt, stirbt die Marke,« *Zeitschrift für Betriebswirtschaftslehre* 1 (2002), suppl. vol., pp. 35–56.

25 *stern MarkenProfile* 10, Nov. 2004.

26 Annual reports of Beiersdorf AG, various years.

27 »Experimente mit den Extras,« *werben & verkaufen*, 18.Oct. 1996, pp. 96–97.

28 »Porsche ist nicht mehr Porsche, wenn uns ein Großer übernimmt,« *brand eins Magazin* 2 (2000).

29 »The Secrets behind McDonald's and Its Hamburgers,« *Business World*, 15. Sept. 2000, p. 31.

30 Upton, David: »McDonald's Corporation (Abridged),« *Harvard Business Online*, 3. Oct. 2003.

31 Hickmann, Craig, and Christopher Raia, »Incubating Innovation: Companies Must Leverage the Full Spectrum of Innovation, from the Incremental to the Revolutionary,« *Journal of Business Strategy*, May 2002, p. 14.

32 »Krise bewältigt – Zauber verloren,« *Die Welt*, 28. Jan. 2005, p. 15; »Marktführer meldet sich zurück,« *Horizont*, 5. May 2005, p. 17.

33 Rücker, Martin, »Der gute Ton macht die Musik,« *Süddeutsche Zeitung*, 19. Nov. 2003, p. 36; »Vivaldi unter der Motorhaube,« *Bonner Generalanzeiger*, 1. March 2003, p. 72.

34 Brandes, Dieter, *Die 11 Geheimnisse des ALDI-Erfolgs* (Frankfurt: Campus Verlag, 2003).

35 »Discounter Lidl wächst abermals schneller als Aldi,« *Die Welt*, 31. May 2005, p. 11; Schlitt, Petra, and Steffen Klusmann, »Angriff des Super-Krämers,« *manager magazin* 9 (2003): p. 38; »Lidl bleibt dem Rivalen Aldi dicht auf den Fersen,« *Financial Times Deutschland*, 21. Oct. 2003, p. 7.

36 See *The Times 100 – Case Studies* (www.tt100.biz).

37 »Japan's Vending Machines Want to Talk to You,« www.thestandard.com, 2. April 2001.

38 »Das Ende der Leidenschaft,« *werben & verkaufen*, 13. Jan. 2005, p. 17.

39 Financial data cited from Club Méditerranée financial reports, www.clubmed.com.

40 Clef, Ulrich, *Die Ausgezeichneten: Unternehmenskarrieren der 30 deutschen Marketing-Preisträger* (München: Clef Creative Communications, 2003): pp. 226, 230.

41 Lau, Peter, »Projekt Bullerbü,« *brand eins Magazin* 3 (2000): pp. 134–139; »IKEA/Skanska: Häuser im Paket,« *Gebäudemanagement*, 1. Oct. 2001, p. 44; »Experienced European Modular Players Eyeing the States,« *Multi-Housing News*, 1. March 2005; IKEA corporate website.

42 At the end of 2003, one year after the start of the campaign, Ikea drew up the balance sheet: the target of 7.5 percent more visitors to the stores had been exceeded by almost 100 percent and customer figures had developed almost as strongly; sales growth had beaten its target of 7.5 percent within one year; and–particularly impressive in terms of efficiency–the advertising budget for 2003, with all the successes, was still EUR 1 million below that of the previous year. See »Effie 2004: Die Sieger. Die Werber meistern schwere Aufgaben,« *Horizont*, 14. Oct. 2004, p. 22.

43 »Stil-Mix wird noch beliebter,« *Horizont*, 13. Nov. 2003, p. 24.

44 See www.katjes.de; »Katjes und Fisherman's nehmen Storcks Riesen in die Zange,« *Handelsblatt*, 26. Jan. 2005, p. 14; »Mittelständler haben zu wenig Vertrauen in die Werbung,« *Frankfurter Allgemeine Zeitung*, 16. Feb. 2004, p. 18.

45 Stuart Crainer, quoted in Klaus Schmeh, *Die 55 größten Flops der Wirtschaftsgeschichte: Krimis, Krisen, Kuriositäten* (Frankfurt: Redline Wirtschaft, 2002): p. 33.

46 Töpfer, Armin, »Rechenfehler im Pentium-Prozessor von Intel im Sommer 1994,« case study, see www.krisennavigator.de.

47 Intel Corporation, *1998 Annual Report*.

48 Clef, Clef, Ulrich, *Die Ausgezeichneten: Unternehmenskarrieren der 30 deutschen Marketing-Preisträger* (München: Clef Creative Communications, 2003)

49 Hirn, Wolfgang and Heide Neukirchen, »Fabrik-Verkauf,« *manager magazin* 11 (2001): pp. 294–302.

2.
Measuring Brands

2.1 The Brand Relevance Tachometer: Assessing the Relative Importance of Brands

From financial services to telecommunications or electricity supply, there is hardly an industry today that does not hope to profit from the growing value of brands. And it is not just in established areas, such as consumer goods, where brands are important. Take retail banking, for instance. In a survey of 6,000 banking customers from ten different European countries, respondents rated the brand as the second most important decision-making criterion (following their proximity to the branch) when choosing a bank. Furthermore, customers are willing to pay higher prices and fees for branded banking services. For a standard commodity, such as a current account, for example, some strong branded banks are able to charge more than twice as much as their lesser competitors. No wonder that in 2003 Peter Wuffli, CEO of UBS, said, »In the financial service industry, a strong brand is critical: it's one of the major factors that attracts clients. Strengthening and simplifying our brand identity and systematically capitalizing on it forms a key part of our organic growth drive.« The success of the UBS brand appears to prove him right: UBS grew its brand value by more than EUR 1 billion from 2004 to 2005.

Though brands are increasingly important, they are not a universal panacea. A closer examination of the business to business (B2B) sector makes this point well. A study by Sattler and PricewaterhouseCoopers reveals that the B2B picture is much more complex than it appears at first sight. Whereas brands represent overall only 18 percent of company value in B2B markets, in the consumer goods segment this figure rises to an average of 53 percent for durable goods and 62 percent for non-durables.[1] In other words, brands are much more relevant to certain businesses than they are to others.

Although the power of brands is certainly increasing, one shouldn't jump blindly onto the brand wagon. If management is not to make serious mistakes, it requires a good understanding of the brand's potential lever effects. The mere assumption that »brands are always important« is misleading and can lead to poor investment decisions. Like all marketing tools, brand investment must be assessed in terms of its potential economic impact and, specifically, on its influence on consumer purchasing behavior. If a brand is unlikely to have a significant impact on consumer behavior, there is little point in making considerable investment in it. Nonetheless, this is a mistake that has been made time and again.

The German electricity sector is a particularly good illustration of how brand recognition does not necessarily translate into a positive impact on the bottom line. Mirroring the consumer goods industry, German electricity suppliers attempted to introduce a number of brands into the market (e.g., RWE produced Avanza, PreussenElektra developed ElektraDirekt, and EnBW introduced Yello). These brands have been relatively successful in securing name recognition at a level similar to that of leading consumer goods companies. However, with the exception of the niche market in »environmentally friendly« electricity, this name recognition has not, until now, induced end-consumers to change their purchasing behavior. This exception is significant, as »green electricity« brands have translated successfully into greater financial returns in a number of electricity companies in the Netherlands and the UK, too.

For private electricity consumers, there are other criteria that they consider more important than the brand in determining their choice of electricity provider. If brands have had any role in shaping the electricity market, it has only been at the local level. Here, surveys indicate that some 80 percent of consumers prefer their electricity to be supplied by their local public utilities company.

This clearly shows that, prior to making any brand investment, it is crucial to have a sound knowledge of the relevance of branding in shaping consumer purchasing in the specific sector in which the company is operating. Making generalizations or abstractions derived from other sectors that might well have little relevance to the sector concerned is likely to lead to poor investment decisions.

Determining brand relevance

The starting point of BrandMatics®, therefore, is that it is necessary to first know how relevant the brand is in shaping purchasing behavior. The brand is only relevant if it can influence the behavior of consumers or intermediate companies.

In order to establish the relative importance of brands to various product segments, McKinsey conducted research into the German business to business (B2B) and business to consumer (B2C) markets in collaboration with

Measuring Brands

a group of researchers from three well-respected German research institutions, the Marketing Centrum Münster at the University of Münster, the Institute for Innovation Research at the University of Kiel, and the Institute for Retail and Marketing at the University of Hamburg.[2] For the purpose of measuring brand relevance, a comprehensive scale was developed and validated according to modern scientific standards. The brand relevance measurement scale not only captures the overall relevance of brands as perceived by customers, but also breaks it down into the three functional components touched on in chapter 1:

- *Information efficiency as the time factor.* Brands make it easier for the consumer to gather and process information about a product.
- *Risk reduction as the trust factor.* Selecting a brand-name product reduces the consumer's (subjective) risk of making a purchase mistake. Brands create trust in the expected performance of the product and provide continuity in the predictability of the product benefit.
- *Image benefit as the expressive factor.* Brands may offer the additional benefit of helping the customer foster a desired image. This benefit can be directed either outward or inward. It is directed outward when the customer uses the brand to cultivate a certain public image. The benefit is directed inward for purposes of self-expression or in identification with certain values and ideals.

The three brand functions cover the entire purchasing and consumption process: information efficiency assists customers prior to the purchase decision, risk reduction influences the actual decision-making activity, and the imaginary benefit emerges in the subsequent consumption phase.

The measurement instrument was applied in two large-scale national and international studies to a broad selection of B2B and B2C markets. The results provide interesting insights that are of high managerial relevance.

The importance of brands in consumer markets across the world

More than 12,000 consumers across the world took part in a representative on-line survey during the summer of 2006.[3] The survey covered 9 countries and 18 product categories. The countries covered were: France, Germany, Japan, Poland, Russia, Spain, Sweden, the United Kingdom, and the United States. The product categories included fast-moving consumer goods, consumer durables, services, and retailers.

Across all countries, cars, beer, and mobile phones belong to the group of product categories where brands show the highest relevance (see fig. 2.1).

Fig. 2.1: Overall relevance ranking in B2C: How important are brands to consumers in different product categories across the world?

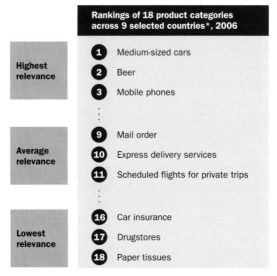

Rankings of 18 product categories across 9 selected countries*, 2006

Highest relevance	1	Medium-sized cars
	2	Beer
	3	Mobile phones
	⋮	
Average relevance	9	Mail order
	10	Express delivery services
	11	Scheduled flights for private trips
	⋮	
Lowest relevance	16	Car insurance
	17	Drugstores
	18	Paper tissues

* Countries in sample: France, Germany, Japan, Poland, Russia, Spain, Sweden, UK, USA
Source: McKinsey

Mail order, express delivery services, and scheduled flights are in the middle of the ranking. Drugstores and tissues constitute the group of product categories that revealed the lowest brand relevance across all countries within the 18 selected categories.

Which brand functions are important for which products?

The survey made it possible to determine the strengths of the selected brand functions in the individual product markets. The combination of these values with the relative importance of the individual brand functions produces the overall brand relevance shown in fig. 2.1. The analysis of consumer evaluations across the nine countries indicates that risk reduction is the most important brand function, followed by the image benefit and the information efficiency function. Analysis of the specific brand functions provides a number of further insights (see fig. 2.2).

Measuring Brands

Information efficiency in the case of recurring purchase decisions

Information efficiency is the dominant brand function in the case of fast-moving consumer goods. The common factors in these markets are: the consumer can select from many brands, the consumer must make a decision relatively quickly, and, of particular relevance, the consumer must make decisions on a regular basis. Accordingly, beer, cigarettes, and detergents are the leading product categories. This is not surprising, considering that cigarette packaging, as an example, consists almost exclusively of brand-defining elements. The situation is similar in such product areas as detergents or beer. Consumers can immediately recognize the brand, which simplifies orientation.

Information efficiency loses importance when the consumer takes more time to make purchase decisions in order to collect information about various offers. This is the case, for instance, with durable consumer goods such as televisions and computers, but also in service sectors, such as car insurance.

Risk reduction for high-end consumer goods

Medium-sized cars are at the top of the ranking for risk reduction, followed by mobile phones and televisions. For drugstores or tissues, risk reduction plays only a secondary role. Even services such as banking are only located in the middle of the list.

Consumers' general desire to minimize the risk associated with purchases accounts for this reasoning. Brands serve as an important pillar of trust in this process. It is easy to understand why consumers want to avoid errors with high-end purchases, such as cars or television; these products demand a fairly large share of the consumer budget. Hence, the financial consequences of a wrong decision are much more severe than in the case of low-budget, fast-moving consumer goods.

Image benefit with publicly displayed products

Not only are medium-sized cars at the top of the ranking for risk reduction, but they are also at the top of the global list in terms of image benefit. They are followed by designer sunglasses and, more surprisingly, mobile network operators. Image benefit is also high across all countries with

Fig. 2.2: Ranking of selected B2C product markets by brand function

Rankings of 18 product categories across 9 selected countries*, 2006			
	Information efficiency	**Risk reduction**	**Image benefit**
Highest relevance — 1	Beer	Medium-sized cars	Medium-sized cars
2	Cigarettes	Mobile phones	Designer sunglasses
3	Medium-sized cars	TV sets	Mobile network operators
⋮			
Average relevance — 9	TV sets	Scheduled flights for private trips	Express delivery services
10	Express delivery services	Designer sunglasses	Scheduled flights for private trips
11	Mail order	Banking accounts	TV sets
⋮			
Lowest relevance — 16	Drugstores	Car insurance	Detergents
17	Car insurance	Drugstores	Drugstores
18	Paper tissues	Paper tissues	Paper tissues

* Countries in sample: France, Germany, Japan, Poland, Russia, Spain, Sweden, UK, USA
Source: McKinsey

respect to mobile phones, beer, and cigarettes. However, as might be expected, the image benefit of drugstores and tissues is of limited relevance.

Image benefit is derived from influencing the perception of others, as well as from one's own identification with the brand. To this extent, the results of the study make sense intuitively. Sunglasses, for instance, are a prestige object visible to all. The same is true for cars and mobile phones. Beer and cigarettes, likewise, possess very specific attributes with which consumers like to be identified.

The results clearly demonstrate that the relevance of brands and the importance of brand functions vary considerably across product markets. Although brands play an important role in consumer decision making in all the countries studied, the question arises whether brands are equally important in every country or if differences exist between countries. The answer to this is important in shaping a company's global marketing strategy.

Brand relevance across countries

Figure 2.3 provides a ranking of the overall brand relevance across the nine selected countries.[4] The United States and two large Eastern European states lead the list. Brands possess the lowest overall relevance in Japan, Sweden, and Germany. Is this ranking useful? We believe it is. It is not surprising that brands have such a high importance in a country such as the United States where the idea of economic freedom has been paramount for a considerable time. It was in there that the principles of modern marketing were born. The conditions there generate highly competitive product markets in which products and services are exchangeable. In this environment, brands play an important role in guiding consumer decisions. In particular, brands help express identity and provide a means of self-expression. In contrast, consumers in Poland and Russia are confronted with a situation that can be characterized by a high level of uncertainty, due to the rapid transition of their economies from a fully planned system to one of liberal markets. Brands are an important means there for reducing uncertainty. Whereas consumers in the former communist states used to be exposed to

Fig. 2.3: Brand relevance ranking across countries: in which countries do consumers focus most on brands?

* Average ranking across all 9 countries and 18 product categories
Source: McKinsey

a very limited choice of product alternatives, under free market conditions the number of alternatives has exploded. Unused to this situation, consumers find information processing challenging. Brands, therefore, serve as a compass to guide consumers through the jungle of products and services.

This helps explain why Poland and Russia lead the country ranking in the functions of information efficiency and risk reduction (see fig. 2.4). The United States heads the list when it comes to the image benefit of brands, followed by Russia and the United Kingdom. Latter is in third position is not surprising. The Hofstede system, which differentiates countries along several cultural dimensions, such as power distance, individualism, and uncertainty avoidance assigns the highest degrees of individualism to the United States and the United Kingdom.[5] Brands are a perfect means of expression in today's individualistic societies.

One may be surprised to find Japan, Sweden, and Germany at the bottom of the ranking lists in fig. 2.3 and 2.4. First of all, it should be noted that although these lists rank countries relative to each other, they do not tell us

Fig. 2.4: Ranking of brand relevance by function across countries: Which brand function is most important?

Deviation from average*	Brand relevance by country and brand function, 2006		
	Information efficiency	Risk reduction	Image benefit
Deviation > +10%	1 Russia 2 Poland 3 USA	1 Russia 2 Poland 3 USA	1 USA 2 Russia
Deviation +/- 10%	4 Spain 5 France	4 France 5 Spain 6 UK	3 UK 4 Poland 5 France 6 Japan 7 Spain
Deviation < -10%	6 Japan 7 UK 8 Germany 9 Sweden	7 Sweden 8 Germany 9 Japan	8 Sweden 9 Germany

* Average ranking across all 9 countries and 18 product categories
Source: McKinsey

anything about the absolute level of brand relevance. The analysis of individual product markets shows that brands are highly relevant to consumer decision making in all three countries, even though this relevance is higher in some countries. In all three, collective values, such as common welfare and a sense of duty, play an important role. In addition, Germans and Japanese are said to be very rational and to strive for perfection. It is probable that these values influence the decision making of consumers in these countries and might explain why brands have a somewhat lesser importance compared to countries such as the United States or Russia. Furthermore, in Germany the importance of discount retailers and private labels has been significantly increasing over the past few years. Thus, in this context, Germany's ranking among these countries is not much of a surprise.

Brand relevance of product categories within countries

We identified that the product categories beer and medium-sized cars lead the list of brand relevance worldwide (see again fig. 2.1). However, this ranking is not uniform across all countries in every product market. For example, the importance of airline brands for private trips varies substantially across countries (see fig. 2.5). In France and Japan, this belongs to the group of categories with the highest relevance, whereas it is in the group with the lowest relevance in the United Kingdom and Sweden. A look at the Hofstede system of cultural characteristics might provide an explanation for this result. French and Japanese societies are very much concerned about uncertainties in life, which they try to avoid. In contrast, the United Kingdom and Sweden score lowest on the uncertainty avoidance scale developed by Hofstede. Airline travel is perceived as risky by many people and sometimes puts extreme psychological pressure on travellers. Brands are an important signal of quality and risk reduction that increases their importance in societies that are more focused on uncertainty avoidance. These intercultural differences regarding brand relevance are also reflected in the success of discount airlines for consumers across different countries. In the United Kingdom and Sweden, where relevance of airline brands for private trips is relatively low, market share of discount airlines is–not surprisingly–relatively high with around 37 percent in the United Kingdom and some 21 percent in Sweden. On the other hand, in Japan for example, a market share of less than one percent for low-cost airlines reflects the relatively high importance of brands in this product category.

Fig. 2.5: Variance of brand relevance across countries in selected product categories

Rank in overall brand relevance among 18 selected product categories	
Scheduled flights for private trips	**Medium-sized cars**
France — 1	France — 2
Germany — 8	Germany — 2
Japan — 4	Japan — 1
Poland — 9	Poland — 2
Russia — 14	Russia — 3
Spain — 15	Spain — 3
Sweden — 17	Sweden — 1
UK — 14	UK — 1
USA — 10	USA — 1

Source: McKinsey

Although brands are equally important across all countries, in certain product markets, such as cars, beer, and cigarettes, this does not generalize to all categories. It is, therefore, necessary to look at each country individually for a specific category in order to identify any differences that might exist in brand leverage.

Brand relevance in Western European countries

The ranking of product categories within the largest three economies of the European Union reveals some significant differences. While cars belong to the highest brand relevance group, in all three countries scheduled flights for private trips and fast-food restaurants are part of this group in France, but not in Germany and the United Kingdom (see fig. 2.6). We have already provided an explanation for the high rank of scheduled flights. The importance of brands in the fast-food business in France, the home of gourmets, appears somewhat unexpected. However, it mirrors the market situation fairly well. One would expect that in markets with high brand relevance for fast food there would be more room for the development of multi

Measuring Brands

Fig. 2.6: Brand relevance by country: How important are brands to consumers across product categories in Western European countries?

Selected rankings of 18 product categories in 3 Western European countries, 2006			
	France	**Germany**	**UK**
Highest relevance 1	Scheduled flights for private trips	Beer	Medium-sized cars
2	Medium-sized cars	Medium-sized cars	Cigarettes
3	Fast-food restaurants	Mobile phones	Beer
⋮			
Average relevance 9	Cigarettes	Scheduled flights for private trips	Department stores
10	Mobile phones	Mail order	Fast-food restaurants
11	Banking accounts	Banking accounts	Designer sunglasses
⋮			
Lowest relevance 16	Detergents	Car insurance	Drugstores
17	Car insurance	Express delivery services	Car insurance
18	Paper tissues	Paper tissues	Paper tissues

Source: McKinsey

ple brands, and this is indeed the case in France, where strong national chains, such as Quick Burger, have been established alongside the dominant American players such as McDonald's and Burger King.

It is no surprise to see that brands are highly relevant to beer consumers in Germany and the United Kingdom. At the bottom of the list, car insurance belongs to the group of categories with the lowest relevance. This is also true for tissues in all three countries. Again, this result for Germany is not too much of a surprise, for when looking closer at the German insurance market, as in car insurance, the market has almost purely been driven by price competition over the last few years.

Brand relevance in the United States and Japan

Different categories head the list of brand relevance in the United States and Japan (see fig. 2.7). In the United States, the importance of brands is especially pronounced in service markets. Express delivery services is

Fig. 2.7: Brand relevance by country: How important are brands to consumers across product categories in the world's largest economies?

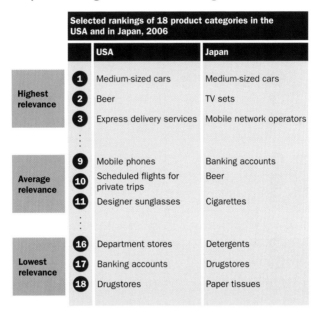

Selected rankings of 18 product categories in the USA and in Japan, 2006		
	USA	**Japan**
Highest relevance (1)	Medium-sized cars	Medium-sized cars
(2)	Beer	TV sets
(3)	Express delivery services	Mobile network operators
⋮		
Average relevance (9)	Mobile phones	Banking accounts
(10)	Scheduled flights for private trips	Beer
(11)	Designer sunglasses	Cigarettes
⋮		
Lowest relevance (16)	Department stores	Detergents
(17)	Banking accounts	Drugstores
(18)	Drugstores	Paper tissues

Source: McKinsey

ranked number three and categories such as mobile network operators and fast-food restaurants are among the top ten categories. As in the United States, brands are highly relevant in Japanese service markets (in such categories as mobile network operators and scheduled flights for private trips), but we also find consumer durables, such as televisions and designer sunglasses, among the categories that have the highest relevance. Japan has strong brands in consumer electronics and this might have contributed to the higher importance of these brands compared to other categories. Japanese customers are among the most valuable customers for luxury goods; the high-ranking position of sunglasses corroborates this observation.

Brand relevance in Eastern European countries

Finally, a comparison of Poland and Russia, two countries whose economies are still emerging from the planned system of former years, provides a number of interesting insights. While cars and mobile phones lead in

Fig. 2.8: Brand relevance by country: How important are brands to consumers across product categories in Eastern European countries?

Selected rankings of 18 product categories in 2 Eastern European countries, 2006		
	Poland	**Russia**
Highest relevance ①	Medium-sized cars	Mobile phones
②	Mail order	Cigarettes
③	Mobile phones	Medium-sized cars
⋮		
Average relevance ⑨	Scheduled flights for private trips	PCs/computers
⑩	Detergents	Express delivery services
⑪	Cigarettes	Fast-food restaurants
⋮		
Lowest relevance ⑯	Fast-food restaurants	Department stores
⑰	Car insurance	Mail orders
⑱	Paper tissues	Paper tissues

Source: McKinsey

both countries, mail order is a category with high brand relevance in Poland but with significantly lower relevance in Russia (see fig. 2.8). Although there are many parallels in the economic and political histories of these two countries, it is not correct to assume that there will be complete consistency in the consumption behavior of the two groups of consumers.

Implications for brand managers

The survey provides a number of important insights into the functioning of consumer markets across the world. First, it should be noted that brands play an important role in many categories irrespective of the country. We identify a remarkable consistency in the high ratings for cars, beers, mobile phones, and cigarettes. International brand managers should continue to pay attention to the development of truly global brands in these categories, such as BMW, Nokia, or Marlboro. Second, brands apparently fulfill important functions in consumer decision making in emerging economies such as Russia and Poland. This observation suggests that despite the lower buying power of their populations, a single focus on a low-price strategy might provide short-term success but is unlikely to be sustainable. Building the brand might well be equally successful in the short term and is likely to establish the roots for future growth. Third, the results reveal considerable differences in brand relevance for categories across countries. Marketing managers can use these insights to identify the countries where brand relevance is highest in order to allocate scarce resources effectively. This will also help managers identify and evaluate the strategy options for the international market entry of new products.

Brand relevance in B2B markets

The significance of brands in the B2B sector has also been investigated comprehensively in market research in cooperation with Professor Backhaus from the Marketing Center Münster (MCM). A total of 769 businesses were surveyed in 2002 in an analysis of 18 German product mar-

Fig. 2.9: Relevance ranking in B2B: How important are brands to business customers?

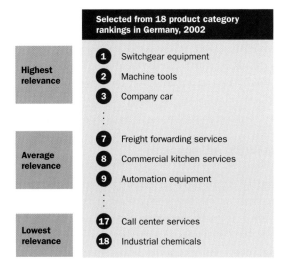

Source: MCM/McKinsey

Measuring Brands

kets. The study yielded results similar to the B2C sector by showing that the relevance of brands varies significantly between product markets.[6] Brand relevance is very strong in switchgear equipment, machine tools, and company vehicles (see fig. 2.9). Brands have the lowest relevance for industrial chemicals; apparently they play a secondary role in such purchases. One surprising result of this analysis is that, for some product markets, the relevance of brands in the B2B sector is rated as high as those in B2C markets. This indicates that there is much untapped potential for B2B branding.

This is not to give the impression, however, that it is sufficient for a business to merely determine brand relevance at the industry-specific level. It is much more important to understand the nature of the functions on which this brand relevance is based on a case-by-case basis. In order to make wise investment decisions, it is necessary to first understand the relative influence of each function and how this applies to certain brands. Not surprisingly, the three brand functions are also highly relevant to the B2B sector, because they reveal interesting aspects of sector-specific brand relevance. Here, brands represent information about a wide range of attributes of the product or service. Brands reduce the degree of complexity and facilitate communication between those involved in the purchase process: buyers, users, and managers.

Information efficiency is strongest for machines and equipment

The information efficiency function of the brand is at its most important for machines and equipment. Such purchases involve complex goods for which brands offer the customer an important orientation aid. For example, by using the »Si« prefix in front of numerous products (e.g., Siematic), Siemens makes orientation easier for its customers; the origin and thus the quality of the product are quickly recognizable. In contrast, the situation is quite different for industrial chemicals or alarm systems, where information efficiency plays only a very secondary role.

Risk reduction is strongest for large-investment products

»Nobody ever got fired for buying IBM,« or so it was said.[7] Opinions differ about this oft-cited statement, but it does serve to highlight the fact that even in the B2B sector brands can minimize the risk of making investment errors. Brands often represent a guarantee of consistent quality, and especially in the area of complex systems, one of compatibility–a strong selling-point of Microsoft programs. In the B2B sector, brands thus provide a crucial function on which to base purchase decisions.

Switchgear equipment and machine tools are products for which risk reduction is the most important brand function. This hardly comes as a surprise, since such equipment is for the most part very expensive and acquired only infrequently. Moreover, this equipment plays a key role in the manufacturing process of the purchasing company, where any equipment failure is likely to have very serious financial consequences. The acquisition of brand-name products is thus a guarantee for process reliability.

Industrial chemicals are commodity products and are purchased relatively frequently. Here the difference between individual brands is marginal. For this reason, brand again plays only a secondary role in risk reduction, and brand relevance is subsequently low in these sectors.

Image benefit is strongest for publicly visible goods

In the B2C sector, the image benefit of a product assists in cultivating the individual consumer's image or in fostering self-expression. In some cases, brand consumption is celebrated by the consumer, for instance, as with designer sunglasses.

Somewhat less obvious is that image benefits are also an important function of brands in the B2B sector, especially in terms of the external representation of the company and its employees. This functions most strongly in the case of publicly visible products and services, such as company cars, shipping companies, or accounting firms. B2B brands are often used as a way of adopting a partner's reputation as part of one's own. This phenomenon of co-branding arises, for instance, among computer manufacturers who advertise with the »Intel inside« logo. The value of a company's own products is enhanced through the image of the worldwide market leader in the computer processor industry.

On the other hand, the public takes little notice of products such as chemicals or alarm systems and so in these sectors the image function is not important. Such goods are found near the end of the image benefit ranking (see fig. 2.10).

As one might expect the average relevance overall of all the brand functions in the B2B domain is somewhat less than in the B2C sector. What might be more surprising is that the gap between the two is not overly large and that brands remain highly significant even for the B2B sector.

Fig. 2.10: Ranking of selected B2B product markets by brand function

Selected rankings of 18 product markets, Germany 2002			
	Information efficiency	**Risk reduction**	**Image benefit**
1	Switchgear equipment	Switchgear equipment	Auditing services
2	Refrigeration equipment	Machine tools	Freight forwarding
3	Machine tools	Company car	Company car
⋮			
7	Fire insurance	Freight forwarding	Production lines
8	Canteen services	Industrial automation	Call center services
9	Call center services	Canteen services	System software
⋮			
17	Alarm systems	Industrial chemicals	Alarm systems
18	Industrial chemicals	Call center services	Industrial chemicals

Source: MCM/McKinsey

Determining brand relevance for non-surveyed markets

McKinsey, with the support of the MCM, developed the McKinsey Brand Relevance Calculator in order to reliably predict brand relevance in all other B2B and B2C markets without resorting to time-consuming and expensive consumer surveys.

The Brand Relevance Calculator is based on the interrelationships ascertained in the study. As an input, the Brand Relevance Calculator requires information derived from a few simple questions, such as what kind of product is involved and how often the product is purchased. Using this information, the calculator then predicts the brand relevance of the market in question on a scale ranging from 0 to 5, including both the general brand relevance and the strength of each individual brand function.

The Brand Relevance Calculator was used to analyze the market for luxury sports cars (see fig. 2.11). Unsurprisingly, image benefit is the dominant brand function here. Luxury sports cars communicate prestige, promote

67

Fig. 2.11: Luxury sports cars: The image benefit increases the brand's relevance significantly

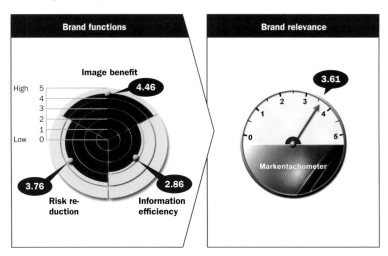

Source: MCM/McKinsey brand relevance survey, GfK

self-expression, and help to cultivate a desired image. The second most important brand function is risk reduction, which is determined by the car's purchase price category, among other factors. Information efficiency, in contrast, is relatively unimportant. This also comes as no surprise, for in making such a purchase, the buyer is normally willing to take considerable time before making a decision.

McKinsey's survey indicated that in the B2C domain of the German electricity market, brand relevance is limited. The question arises whether this is also true for business users, or whether it might make better sense for electricity providers to invest in brand building in the corporate market. That this is indeed the case is supported by the fact that significantly stronger brand relevance was observed in the B2B sector (between corporate customers and public utility companies). Here electricity is ranked in the middle of the list overall. Its brand relevance derives primarily from the risk reduction function, producing a value of approximately 2.5. The explanation for this is that corporate customers are concerned with minimizing any significant risk that might cause a stoppage in their production. The reliability promised by a well-respected brand is, therefore, a competitive factor. This reveals that there are clear opportunities for brand building in the electricity market, as long as the focus is on the corporate customer rather than on the general consumer.

Implications for management

What lessons can be learned from these findings? The significance of brands for corporate success is indisputable, but this study on brand relevance shows that because the leverage effect of brands varies from market to market, brand building is not likely to have the same impact in all cases. Companies first need to analyze what relevance brands possess in specific markets, as well as the reasons for this pertinence. It is important to note that brands target several markets simultaneously (e.g., B2B, B2C, capital market, recruiting, etc.). It is therefore important to analyze the brand relevance in each individual segment.

Where there is market saturation in the end-consumer market, an analysis of brand relevance can help to avoid serious investment mistakes. In the B2B sector in particular, brand relevance analysis reveals that there are a number of significant market opportunities that companies have yet to capture.

2.2 Market Segmentation: Identifying and Selecting the Right Target Groups

Brand relevance analysis provides management with a clear indication of what the likely impact will be of building a brand in a specific market environment. It is important to keep in mind, however, that the results are only valid for a specific sector or a certain product market, not for a single company or even a single brand, the relevance of which may vary by segment.

Again, the German electricity industry provides us with an interesting example of why, despite its overall low brand relevance, a number of niche products in the private energy market, such as Lichtblick, Naturstrom, and NaturEnergie, have succeeded in establishing themselves as electricity brands. The relevant market in this case is not the German electricity market, which is made up of large-scale providers such as E.ON and RWE. Instead, these niche brands use a brand promise that is primarily ecological in order to target their market for »environmentally friendly energy.« Analysis of this market indicates significantly higher brand relevance, especially in terms of information efficiency and image benefit. Moreover, many consumers are willing to pay a premium for »clean« energy. According to market research, 37 percent of German customers and 46 percent of British say they will pay up to 10 percent extra for it. Companies are therefore looking for ways to validate the green credentials of their brand, trust being one of the key brand drivers in this niche market. In the Netherlands, for example, distribution companies such as Nuon and Essent sell »green electricity« with the verification of the Dutch branch of the World Wide Fund for Nature.

The coffee filter machine market provides another example of the need to examine the brand relevance in the relevant market segment, rather than looking at the market in its entirety. Overall, filter coffee machines are still a commodity with a low brand relevance score of 2.02. Yet certain brands have managed to differentiate themselves and have created a high-value segment by providing upscale luxury machines with elegant designs (e.g., Jura or Saeco), or by new innovations that focus on convenience (e.g., Senseo's use of cup-size pads). Analysis shows that for these market segments, the image benefit and information efficiency functions play a much more important role than for the general market.

Even if the analysis of brand relevance does indeed lead to the decision to invest in brand development, management faces the task of developing a full understanding of the relevant brand environment before deciding on the nature and form of its own brand strategy. At this stage, BrandMatics® requires a detailed definition of the brand image and a quantitative analysis of its brand strength within the competitive environment of the target market. A thorough analysis of the brand image starts with the segmentation of the relevant market, keeping two goals in mind: first, the need to identify those segments that are attractive in general and, second, to then select the most suitable target groups for the individual business and the brand promise (see fig. 2.12).[8]

It is often argued that the job of a business is to produce products or services that appeal to all people as potential customers. If this were true, it would make the identification of target groups less relevant. We believe that this is a major misconception, however. Consumers are no longer a homogenous group and cannot be treated as such. Greater wealth has created greater choice and this has ensured that today's societies are highly differentiated in both their aspirations and consumption patterns. And this differentiation is increasing. However, differentiation is taking place at the same time as globalization, so there are emerging commonalities that cut across national markets. The right way to think of consumers, therefore, is no longer as one single mass market but as a range of consumer groups, all of whom have differing aspirations and demands–regardless of whether we are talking of rail travel, mail services, department stores, insurance, or even the consumption of bread from the local bakery. These consumer groups may well cross national boundaries (as in music and youth fashion),

Fig. 2.12: Market segmentation using two simple questions

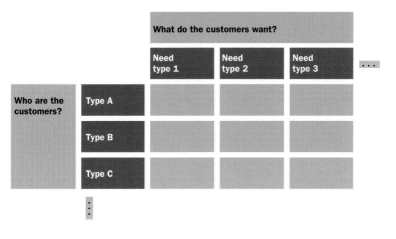

Source: McKinsey

but it is also true that they are not homogenising at the national level. Certainly in Europe, the vast majority of men and women and children will at some time travel by rail or visit a department store; all age groups receive letters and have insurance needs; and all income groups do, however occasionally, buy bread. The difference is in the expectations and demands of the different segments–and this is increasing. It is as true as ever that »you can't please all of the people all of the time.« Segmenting the market and identifying the right target groups are thus critical tasks for every brand, in every market.

Market segmentation needs to be approached as a strategic task, one that encompasses and focuses the activity of the entire company. Externally, customer-focused companies use market segmentation to produce a credible and consistent brand presence; internally, they use it to produce rapid, clear-sighted decisions directed towards the common goal of meeting the needs of their selected target customers in an optimal and profitable manner.

First task: identifying target groups

The principle of customer need and benefit has been applied in the research and practice of market segmentation for many decades. According to Haley (1968), the benefit associated with a product or service and perceived by the (potential) customer represents the basis for defining internally homogeneous customer segments with similar needs. Regardless of how a customer benefit is determined and measured in the individual case,[9] it is clear that it should play a major role in segmentation. In certain circumstances, this variable may be replaced by purchase motivations, attitudes, or personal values, since these attributes are methodologically similar to consumer needs. The benefit variable is essential in determining target segments effectively, and these in turn are the basis for deriving conclusions about how all elements of the marketing mix should be defined.

This is only the initial basis for customer segmentation. The task of segmentation is further complicated by the increasing variety of products, the influence of the media, and the convergence of technologies. Increasingly, this allows customers to vary their behavior–and this is exactly what they do. Customers often do not decide which brand to buy until they reach the location of purchase. Designer fashion is being combined with own-brand labels and luxury cars can be seen parked at discount supermarkets. Customers are becoming more comfortable with making use of a multiplicity of options and as a result, their behavior is more difficult to predict.

The need/benefit approach needs, therefore, to be amended to include these additional factors, such as taking account of the variety of potential consumption options, reasons for purchase, or even demographic variables, depending on the market. For instance, travellers may be more price-conscious when travelling for personal reasons, but more concerned with saving time on business trips. Even a gourmet consumer sometimes eats convenience food when in a hurry or when alone. Parents may buy products for themselves at discount retailers, but shop for their children at organic groceries. Customer needs and their associated behavior are, therefore, situation specific. The situation, because it has such a powerful influence over behavior, provides the context for understanding this behavior.

The task of segmentation can thus be summarized as follows: similar customers with similar needs are grouped together and related to the situational context of product usage or purchase.

Defining market segments based on benefit expectations is indisputably effective, but it is also inefficient. Marketing is often mistakenly understood as purely that of the best possible satisfaction of customer needs. This is to forget that the satisfaction of customer needs is, after all, simply a means to an end in terms of sales–that of maximizing demand and stimulating a willingness to purchase. In other words, superior marketing concepts must be both effective and efficient. The world's best target group solution is useless if the customer segments it identifies are unapproachable in terms of marketing, because they cannot be reached efficiently through a series of advertisements or a targeted sales strategy.

Our experience indicates that the »dilemma of market segmentation«[10] can best be solved by combining segmentation criteria. This combination can be represented in a »need-state« segmentation matrix, in which customer need is combined with situational or »approachability« factors (e.g., receptiveness, availability, and need for interaction). The need/benefit variable here indicates how brands should be defined; the market appeal is oriented towards the approachability dimension. In practice, this can be made use of in a number of ways. The situational factors mentioned above, such as the purpose of travel in the travel services sector,[11] often prove to be important indicators for describing various customer types, for instance, in terms of their different approaches to acquiring information. Alternatively, simple demographic criteria can be employed, such as in the example of a benefit segmentation in the financial services sector in Figure 2.13.

Primary market research and analysis offers sophisticated methods for data collection that can be used to identify potential segments. Many

---

Fig. 2.13: Two practical segmentation examples (in percent)

Financial services	High-end service	Medium intensity service	Low-end service
Conservative/ older	2	16	36
Progressive/ younger	9	19	18

Rail travel	Speed-oriented	Price-sensitive	Comfort-oriented
Business trip	12	12	6
Private trip	15	33	10
Commuter trip	4	6	2

Source: McKinsey

researchers favor conjoint analyses for understanding dimensions of need. The most common techniques are computer-aided methods of adaptive conjoint analysis (ACA) and choice-based conjoint analysis (CBC). These methods use trade-off decisions to force customers to give realistic answers. In addition, relatively new approaches, such as hierarchical individualized limit conjoint analysis (HILCA), take individual decision-making mechanisms into consideration.[12] Newer qualitative techniques, such as ethnographic observation, are also gaining ground as a method by which to understand the situational context. These techniques are beginning to displace the classic group and focus discussions. These new approaches take the social and cultural context into consideration, eliminating earlier weaknesses, such as problems in articulation and the influences of the interviewer on the interviewee.

Users might not be uninterested in the relative merits or methodological details of the individual approaches, but they do need to be interested in achieving a reasonable cost-benefit ratio in the implemented solution. This often leads them to reject conjoint approaches, regardless of how superior they might be, due to the time and expense that is required to conduct the initial primary survey. In many cases this rejection is justified; suitable data is often already available in the company but has simply been ignored or not analyzed properly.

Many companies are unaware of the wealth of data they possess from previous qualitative market research. This data, combined with scanner data, transaction data, information from loyalty programs, and click streams in the Internet, can provide an abundance of valuable information. By using new analysis techniques that combine data, or by systemizing data collection, an understanding of their customers and their multi-option behavior can be acquired. This can then be used as the basis for targeted market development without having to carry out extensive primary surveys.

A number of companies have already taken advantage of modern data management. The financial services provider Capital One, for instance, invested substantially in data management in the 1990s, linking survey data with transaction and loyalty data and thus grouping several million customers into thousands of tactical segments that could be targeted through direct marketing. Capital One possesses a 2 MB volume of information on each customer. The result of this investment has been that its number of customers has grown continually, increasing by 50 percent a year from 1992 to 2004. N. Morris, the co-founder of Capital One, describes the company's customer orientation in this manner: »We are an information-based marketing company, not a credit card issuer ... we're making Capital One a branded customer-centric company.«[13]

Not every company has been as successful in collecting and analyzing information on customer behavior. This leaves them vulnerable. The ability to generate and analyze data in a targeted manner contributes significantly to long-term corporate success. Our experience indicates that a successful market strategy, based on systematic segmentation of (potential) customers, generates on average a 10 percent increase in the volume of sales.

From segmentation to target groups

Segmentation is not just about understanding customer behavior. For it to be efficient, segmentation must also be comprised of a strategic component that pays due regard to economics. Not every segment is equally lucrative. Nor, typically, will a brand appeal equally to all segments. As a result, developing the different segments will involve varying levels of investment in each segment.

Fig. 2.14: Segmentation example

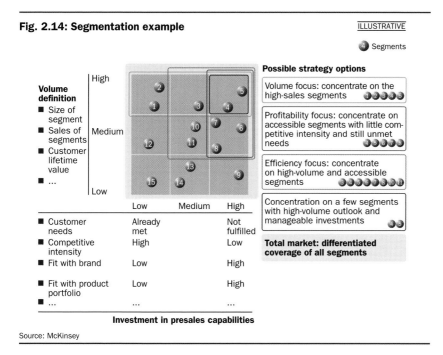

Source: McKinsey

Measuring Brands

Faced with inevitable limitations in their resources, brand managers are faced with deciding which segments they should prioritize and how best to develop marketing to those so prioritized. To answer this, the volume significance of each segment first needs to be examined. The key parameters here are the size of the segment, the intensity of use, and what is known as the »customer lifetime value.« The investments necessary to acquire the segment must also be considered; decisive factors here include the intensity of competition, medial availability, and congruence between brand and products (see fig. 2.14). A smaller segment with less intense competition might turn out to be a more efficient investment than a larger, more hotly disputed one.

Depending on the company's initial situation, a range of strategies for segment development are possible:

Volume focus: Marketing is focused on the large segments that offer high revenue.

Profitability focus: Focus is on the segments that are more easily approached, where there is less intense competition and unfulfilled consumer needs, and where the current brand already appeals to the corresponding segments.

Efficiency focus: Focus simultaneously on several high-volume, approachable segments.

Concentration strategy: Concentration on focused investments in a few segments with high volume potential.

Total market strategy: Invest in differentiated, simultaneous development of all segments.

Because segment development strategies differ in the amount of resources they require, selecting the most suitable strategy will depend on the availability of financial and human resources. Developing all segments equally in a total market strategy is likely to require very significant investments in products, channels and, of course, brand management and communication; prioritization is therefore important (this is explored further in section 3.3 on the brand portfolio).

Characteristics of a good segmentation

For a segmentation to be successful in its execution it needs to be both robust and practical. Even the most sophisticated segmentation is of little use if the resulting target groups are not embedded in the company's structures and processes.

A robust and practical segmentation has the following characteristics:
- The segments are distinct from one another in terms of brand and product preferences.
- The segmentation provides evidence of untapped customer needs.
- It is possible to use a medial appeal to reach these segments.
- The segment names relate clearly to the market, are easy to comprehend, and the total number of segments is manageable.

Keeping things practical in terms of implementation is of key importance. Consulting firms and market research institutes often try to outdo one another with innovative and creative solutions in market segmentation. Frequently what emerges is a target group solution that may please the academic or the head of market research, but which has little practical use in day-to-day management decisions. Currently, because direct, one-to-one marketing remains an elusive if not impossible goal in many industries, there is no practical alternative to marketing to target groups. This makes it all the more important to bridge the gap between ensuring the validity of the segmentation and methodological sophistication on the one hand, and taking into account the practical considerations of how the segmentation is to be embedded in all levels of the company on the other. In segmentation, less is more.

2.3 The Brand Diamond: Developing a Precise Understanding of Brand Image

As soon as the market segments have been determined and the target groups that are likely to prove the most attractive have been identified, the next step is to ascertain the image of the brand.

As described in the first chapter, strong brands generate an unmistakable image in the minds of consumers. It is important for the company to fully understand the nature of this image in terms of how and why it influences the consumer. This provides the basis for assessing how management can develop this image further to trigger the decision to purchase. Success in influencing behavior in this manner will increase the value of the brand.[14]

In marketing science, both the foundations and the creation of brand image have been studied extensively.[15] Numerous approaches have been developed based on behavioral science and with the aid of brand equity research, which seek to understand and structure brand associations.[16] Nearly all these concepts feature a hierarchical structure that differentiates

Fig. 2.15: A holistic perspective on brands: The McKinsey brand diamond

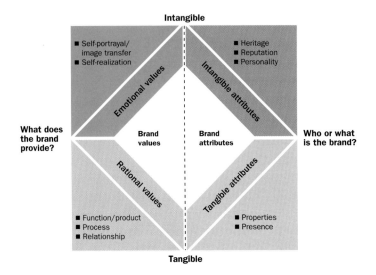

Source: McKinsey

between attributes, benefit perceptions formed from these attributes, and the resulting global attitudes or associations.[17]

McKinsey has developed its own empirically-based structuring approach for analyzing brand image. Using this method, the attribute and benefit associations of a brand image can be divided into four elements. These include the factors that are inherent in the brand, independent of its consumption, and the benefits it provides to the consumer. This yields the brand diamond, which represents all the associations linked to a brand and their relationship with each other (see fig. 2.15).

Tangible factors: The associations in this category are generally those that arise first in the perception of the consumer. This category includes all the characteristics that can be perceived by the senses, forming the basis for the strength of a brand's image in the minds of consumers. They can be physical or functional in nature, such as engine horsepower or product design, as well as those related to a brand's presentation, for instance, as communicated in advertising or promotional campaigns.

Intangible factors: The intangible factors comprise all the characteristics associated with a brand's origin, reputation, and personality that cannot be sensed directly but are nonetheless important to the consumer's understanding of the brand. These include associations such as »a brand with tradition« or »an innovative brand.« The intangible brand factors typically build on tangible ones. The image of the cowboy in Marlboro's brand presence, for instance, triggers associations of freedom and adventure. Today, these intangible attributes are probably much more important for Marlboro's image than any tangible ones.

Rational benefits: All the measurable benefits the brand brings the consumer fall into this category. Rational benefits can be expressed in the product or its function (e.g., comfortable seats), the transaction process (convenient transaction handling), or in the relationship of the consumer to the brand or provider (good consultation from friendly staff). Rational benefits are directly related to tangible brand factors. A high-speed train, for instance, offers the rational benefit of reduced travel time.

Emotional benefits: Consumers associate an emotional benefit with a brand if it reinforces their personal self-image (image transfer) or self-expression. Brands can be used in this manner as status symbols that provide them with prestige, a Porsche sports car being a good example.

The brand diamond can be used to fully analyze the brand image in three steps. The first step is to determine all the relevant or potentially relevant brand associations in the pertinent market environment. The four dimensions of the brand diamond act as a structural aid that helps to ascertain accurately all the attributes influencing the brand image. These attributes are identified through interviews or in the course of preliminary quantitative market research. The old adage of »garbage in, garbage out« applies here, of course. If factors that are important in influencing the brand image are not measured adequately or are neglected completely, then there is a high risk of producing an incorrect conclusion. This is particularly true in analyzing the emotional benefits of the brand (the upper left edge of the brand diamond). In the B2B sector, for instance, many companies have reservations about addressing the emotional benefits of the brand (»We're talking about the forklift market, where the only thing that matters is what it can do and what it costs!«). Despite such misconceptions, a detailed analysis demonstrates how strongly the brand effect depends on the dimension of emotional benefit. These are revealed in such forms as »a brand you can trust,« »one can depend on it,« or »it fits my company.« Typically, a total of 20 to 50 image dimensions are taken into consideration in a brand image analysis. Selecting the right number for the brand is a trade-off between the costs (of the market research) and benefits (gained through additional knowledge).

Fig. 2.16: Brand diamond: Mercedes C-Class vs. VW Passat

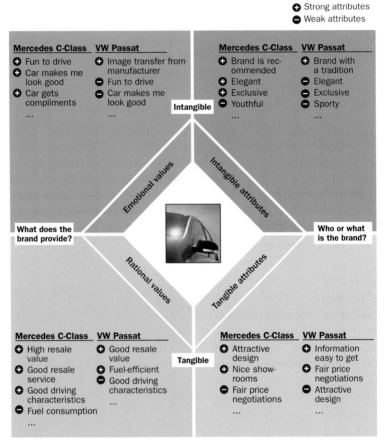

⊕ Strong attributes
⊖ Weak attributes

Mercedes C-Class	VW Passat
⊕ Fun to drive	⊕ Image transfer from manufacturer
⊕ Car makes me look good	⊖ Fun to drive
⊕ Car gets compliments	⊖ Car makes me look good
...	...

Intangible

Mercedes C-Class	VW Passat
⊕ Brand is recommended	⊕ Brand with a tradition
⊕ Elegant	⊖ Elegant
⊕ Exclusive	⊖ Exclusive
⊕ Youthful	⊖ Sporty
...	...

Emotional values

Intangible attributes

What does the brand provide?

Who or what is the brand?

Rational values

Tangible attributes

Mercedes C-Class	VW Passat
⊕ High resale value	⊕ Good resale value
⊕ Good resale service	⊕ Fuel-efficient
⊕ Good driving characteristics	⊖ Good driving characteristics
⊖ Fuel consumption	...
...	

Tangible

Mercedes C-Class	VW Passat
⊕ Attractive design	⊕ Information easy to get
⊕ Nice show-rooms	⊕ Fair price negotiations
⊖ Fair price negotiations	⊖ Attractive design
...	...

Source: INRA consumer survey, Germany 2002, McKinsey

Once the image dimensions have been selected, the second step is to have these dimensions evaluated by (potential) customers in a quantitative market research study. The images of the essential brands are generally measured with the help of rating scales.

The third and final step is to compare the image of the company's own brand with that of competing brands. In principle, it would be possible to make a comparison for each of the dimensions of brand image. However, in order to avoid an exceedingly high degree of complexity (and cost) it is better to make a comparison of only those dimensions in which the brand possesses critical strengths or weaknesses.

It is helpful to look at how the brand diamond works in practice. In an outside-in independent market research study in 2002, McKinsey used the brand diamond to analyze the Mercedes C-Class in comparison with the VW Passat. From the results, it is evident that the Mercedes brand was clearly superior to that of the Passat in the emotional dimensions. Apparently, the Passat had not yet succeeded in completely shedding its image of being somewhat unexciting. Figure 2.16 provides an illustration of the use of the brand diamond in comparing the Volkswagen Passat and Mercedes C-Class on select image dimensions.

As this example illustrates, a brand typically elicits several categories of association. The tangible brand attributes, for instance, might include a superior product concept or a creative advertising presence, which might derive directly from the rational benefits of the brand. Though these are critical elements in a brand's success, an analysis of more than 100 brand diamonds in some 20 market environments confirms that the secret to the success of strong brands lies in the combination of rational and emotional benefits, as the leading brands demonstrate. Successful brand management needs to recognize this principle, regardless of whether the brand is in confectionery, the detergent market, or the steel industry.

Nivea: Emotions make the difference

Nivea is a good example of a strong brand. Its story has been one of outstanding success The share price of its parent company Beiersdorf is one indication of this achievement. In contrast to the share price of its competitors, which lost on average a fifth of their value between 2000 and 2002, Beiersdorf's share price nearly doubled in the same period. A significant proportion of this gain can be attributed to Beiersdorf's power brand, Nivea.

When Nivea started in the German market in 1911, the brand represented a simple moisturizing cream. It was not until the 1980s that the first new product lines were introduced, with substantial expansion in the 1990s. Today, products such as NIVEA Beauté or NIVEA Hair Care can be found in almost every supermarket across the world.

This raises the question, of course, as to why Nivea has been so extraordinarily successful in the ongoing expansion of its product lines. The answer can be illustrated using the example of Nivea shampoo in Germany. Although the German shampoo market is highly competitive, in a very short period Nivea succeeded in capturing a market share of approximately 11 percent—more than competing brands Timotei, Poly Kur, and Vivality combined.[18] Despite developments in the market in recent years, in which customers have become increasingly price conscious, contributing to the explosive growth of own-label supermarket brands, Nivea's market share has never been threatened.

Nivea's success is the result of a distinct, strongly emotional brand image, as illustrated by the brand diamond for NIVEA Hair Care (see fig. 2.17) surveyed in an independent market research with German consumers.

Fig. 2.17: The brand diamond also reflects the emotional side of Nivea

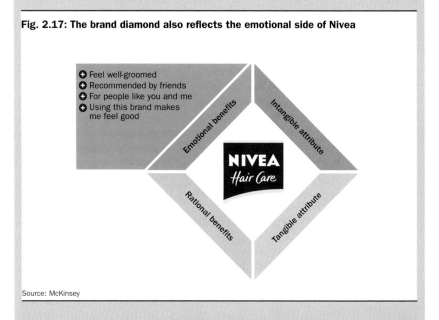

Source: McKinsey

Of course, Nivea offers more than just emotions; it also delivers rational product attributes such as gentle and effective cleansing. This, however, is also true of its competitors' brands. Nivea's success is built on its emphasis on the emotional brand attributes. Consumers attribute such characteristics to Nivea shampoos as the »brand for people like you and me.« Other image attributes important to the purchase process include »I feel well-groomed with this brand« and »recommended by friends.« Nivea's competitive advantage lies in its strong emotional profile. Strong brands evoke strong emotions.

Once the brand diamond has been used to reveal all the associations linked to a brand, the next task is to shape the brand image in the desired direction. For this purpose, it is important to gain a quantitative understanding of how a consumer's image of the brand influences his or her behavior.

2.4 The Brand Purchase Funnel: Measuring and Quantifying Brand Performance

The crucial question that needs to be answered in quantifying the performance of the brand is how the brand image and consumer attitude influence purchase behavior. These aspects can be quantitatively measured and assessed; this is the core of BrandMatics®.

Establishing a correlation between the brand image and the attitudes and behavior of consumers is vital for the successful development and management of brands. But management often underestimates this aspect. In many cases, awareness of brands and global image value remain the exclusive indicator of brand success. These two criteria are even reflected nowadays in the business targets of the senior management of top companies, despite the fact that neither brand awareness nor global image value says anything about the actual economic success of the brand.

Measuring brand performance using the brand purchase funnel

A brand's impact on behavior can be measured using the brand purchase funnel (also referred to here as the brand funnel). This is based on the AIDA model (Attention, Interest, Desire, Action) from the realm of behavioral science. It represents the purchase process in five typical, idealized stages: What percentage of the target group is 1) aware of the brand? 2) is familiar with its products and services prior to deciding to buy? 3) will consider the brand for purchase? 4) have already purchased it once? and 5) would purchase it again, that is, are loyal customers? Strong brands tend to be successful at all stages: they achieve a high degree of awareness, are included in the consideration set, are purchased, and finally convert buyers into loyal customers. The last two stages of the brand funnel are crucial; this is where consumer behavior has a direct impact on the level of sales and earnings.

In order to measure the performance of a brand in the brand funnel, market research data on consumer behavior is collected at each stage.

Fig. 2.18: Applying the brand funnel to cars

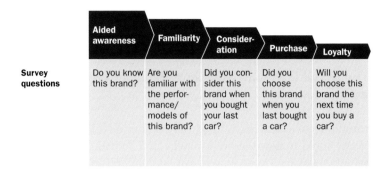

	Aided awareness	Familiarity	Consideration	Purchase	Loyalty
Survey questions	Do you know this brand?	Are you familiar with the performance/ models of this brand?	Did you consider this brand when you bought your last car?	Did you choose this brand when you last bought a car?	Will you choose this brand the next time you buy a car?

Source: MCM/McKinsey

Using this data it is possible to calculate the respective number of customers the brand retains from stage to stage. Figure 2.18 illustrates the schematic operation of the brand funnel in the automobile sector.

The brand funnel can, in principle, be applied to any B2B or B2C market, though it will need to be adapted to the sector under investigation. The number and structure of the stages will vary by industry. It is useful to look at a number of examples to see how this can be done. In the case of fast-moving consumer goods sectors, for example, in goods such as cigarettes, shampoo, or mineral water, the »will consider« stage can be replaced or supplemented by »trial purchase.« In this way, occasional purchases of the products can be reflected accurately, as these are important to the brand. In the case of financial investments, the stages of »ownership« and »main investment« (loyalty) would be integrated into the final stages of the purchase funnel. When applying the purchase funnel to the retail domain, the first stages would include »visiting the shop« or »visiting the store department.« The brand funnel can even be employed in non-business environments, for instance, in analyzing commitment to political parties. In this case, the final »purchase« and »repeat purchase« stages of the funnel would be replaced by »have voted for« and »will vote for again.«

Due to its broad foundation in behavioral science, purchase funnel analysis has been applied in marketing practice for some considerable time and is now a well-accepted tool for nearly all agencies and management consulting firms. It is important to note that despite fundamental similarities, the approaches often differ in the number of stages that are included in the funnel. This is important, for the number of stages determines the »effect hierarchy« that is under investigation. Even more important is that many users concentrate only on the absolute values in the process stages. But such an interpretation yields few meaningful results, since the absolute values of the process stages at the beginning of the purchase funnel–such as a high degree of awareness or familiarity–can be »purchased« through sufficiently extensive advertising campaigns. More important from a management point of view is the conversion rates, which can be derived from the absolute values of the process stages. These indicate at which points in the purchase process a brand loses potential customers, thus revealing bottlenecks in the purchase process. This serves to make management aware of weak points in the funnel, as well as helping to focus investment on the most effective levers.

This interrelationship is illustrated using the example of the Volkswagen Passat dating from the year 2002 (see fig. 2.19).[19] As can be seen, nearly 100 percent of the surveyed group were aware of the VW Passat. As would have been expected, at each successive stage of the purchase funnel the brand lost (potential) customers; at the end only 8 percent of those surveyed remained loyal VW Passat customers. At first sight, this appears to be a low level of customer loyalty.

It is hard to interpret these figures meaningfully, however, until they are compared with a rival brand. A comparison with the Mercedes C-Class, in 2002, when the survey was conducted (see fig. 2.20) confirms that, as was

---

Fig. 2.19: The brand performance of the VW Passat in the purchase funnel
(in percent)

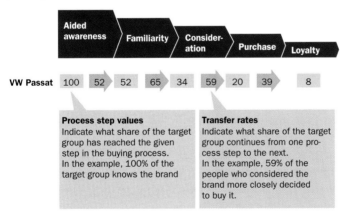

Fig. 2.20: The funnel highlights the VW Passat's brand weaknesses in 2002 (in percent)

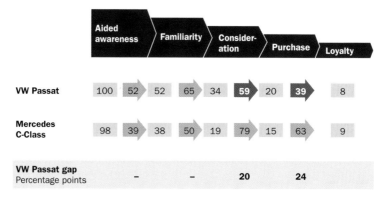

	Aided awareness		Familiarity		Consideration		Purchase		Loyalty
VW Passat	100	52	52	65	34	59	20	39	8
Mercedes C-Class	98	39	38	50	19	79	15	63	9
VW Passat gap Percentage points		–		–		20		24	

Source: MCM/McKinsey, 2002

first suspected, the loyalty rate for the VW Passat was indeed weak. Whereas the Passat succeeded in converting only 39 percent of purchasers to the »loyalty« stage, the Mercedes C-Class secured a much higher conversion rate, that of 63 percent. Given its narrower target market with customers willing to pay more for their car, the Mercedes C-Class was likewise superior in converting customers from the »consideration« stage to »purchase,« with an edge of 20 percentage points over VW. It was therefore clear from this that the Mercedes C-Class was significantly more successful than the VW Passat in turning potential customers into actual buyers or loyal repeat customers. In the light of Mercedes' strong performance in the final stages of the purchase funnel, the fact that it slightly trailed the Passat in the initial process stages hardly matters in the end.

Examples of the application of the brand purchase funnel

The power of the brand purchase funnel can be illustrated using various examples from a range of industries.

Mobile phones: The German mobile phone market provides a good example of how systematic, data-driven brand analysis can strongly support the assessment of a brand's performance and provide brand managers with valuable indicators for potential success or failure. In Germany, the market for mobile phones was dominated for the most part by Nokia, followed by competitor brands such as Motorola, Sony Ericsson, BenQ-Siemens, and Samsung. Over the past five years, the Korean Samsung brand has managed to continuously increase its market share to around 15 percent in 2005, and hopes to continue to shrink the still very sizeable gap from market leader Nokia in the coming years.

The results of outside-in market research conducted in summer 2006 show that the two brands Samsung and Nokia, enter the purchase process with the same degree of product awareness; both are at 98 percent. But already in the conversion to the »familiarity« stage, Nokia takes a clear lead, the gap between the two brands at this stage being 16 percent. This means that (potential) customers are apparently more familiar with Nokia-brand mobile phones than with those from Samsung. This is probably due in part to Nokia's advantage as the specialized market leader. Whereas consumers associate Nokia almost exclusively with high-performance mobile telephones, the Samsung brand name is linked with numerous other products and services as well, including flat screen TVs and washing machines. Beyond the lever of brand familiarity, Nokia succeeds in converting 56 percent of those who consider buying a Nokia mobile phone into people who view Nokia as their favorite handset brand. At this stage Samsung achieves a conversion rate of just 23 percent, some 33 percentage points behind Nokia – resulting in the biggest gap along the funnel (see fig. 2.21).

Tobacco: An example from the Spanish cigarette market, based on McKinsey research carried out in 2005, illustrates how the brand funnel approach needs to be adapted depending on the sector or product market that is to be analyzed. Here, the »purchase« stage is divided into »trial/purchase« and »frequent purchase« in order to integrate occasional buyers of the brand into the analysis (see fig. 2.22). With an awareness of almost 100 percent, Camel and the domestic brand Fortuna are as well known as the global market leader Marlboro. Furthermore, both Camel's and Fortuna's performance along the first four stages of the funnel, from brand awareness to familiarity, consideration, and trial/purchase are also only a little behind that of Marlboro. It is the distinction between trial/purchase and frequent purchase in the brand funnel that reveals the actions the cigarette brands need to take. Camel obviously fails to convert customers from »trial/purchase« to »frequent purchase.« The same is true for Fortuna, which converts only

Fig. 2.21: Brand funnel analysis in mobile phones
(results in percent)

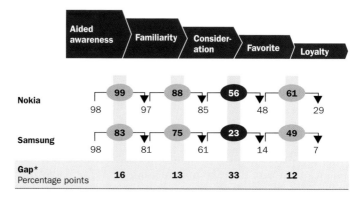

* Versus the benchmark
Source: McKinsey German consumer survey, 2006

Fig. 2.22: Brand funnel analysis in tobacco (in percent)

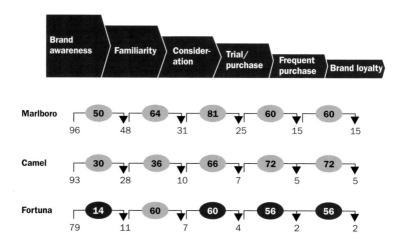

Source: McKinsey Spanish market research, April 2005 (n = 501)

Measuring Brands

slightly more customers (37 percent compared to Camel's 30 percent). Clearly, both brands need therefore to focus their marketing efforts on this bottleneck if they are to gain market share against Marlboro.

Tourism: A further example of the flexibility of the brand purchase funnel's application is demonstrated in its use in assessing competing tourist destinations (see fig. 2.23). A market research study carried out in Germany in 2004 examined the various stages of the purchase funnel for holiday destinations in Austria and Switzerland. This analysis showed that for German tourists Austrian destinations are well ahead of Swiss ones. The major reason why is found in the front end of the purchasing funnel. In response to the question, »Do you know any Austrian tourist destinations?« 71 percent of those surveyed answered »yes,« while only 58 percent said they knew Swiss ones. Similarly, the conversion rate from »familiarity« to »consideration« is 11 percentage points higher for Austria as a destination than for Switzerland. To counter this, Switzerland needs to invest in its tourism marketing in order to build familiarity with its destinations. One interesting aspect of the analysis is that it shows comparatively high loyalty rates for those who have already visited Swiss holiday destinations. This indicates that so-called taster offers aimed at potential tourists who have already been to Switzerland might well be successful in diverting tourism from Germany.

Fig. 2.23: The brand funnel is a highly versatile analytical tool – tourism example (in percent)

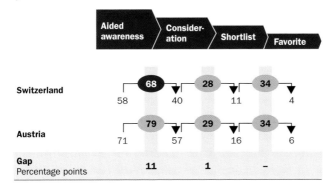

Source: McKinsey survey conducted in Germany, 2005

Once the brand funnel has been used to identify the gaps in the brand in comparison to its relevant competitors, the next stage potentially is to invest in fixing those gaps. McKinsey has developed its brand potential method in cooperation with the Marketing Center Münster (MCM) in order to invest effectively in building and expanding a brand. The brand potential method can be used to quantify the potential sales improvement derived from improved conversion rates.

In calculating a brand's sales potential, it is important to realize that at any stage of the purchase funnel, consumer behavior is not only the result of brand impact but also the interplay of all elements of the marketing mix. For instance, the VW Passat's high conversion rate from the awareness stage to the familiarity stage when compared to the Mercedes C-Class (52 percent versus 39 percent; see fig. 2.20) is more likely to originate from the significant price difference between the two automobiles than from the nature of the brand. In other words, in order to determine the brand potential, it is first necessary to extract the impact derived purely from the brand from that arising from other elements in the marketing mix. Only when the impact of the brand has been isolated in this way is it possible to determine what potential contribution the brand can make towards closing gaps in the rate of conversions.

The McKinsey brand potential method makes such calculations possible using a multivariate analysis technique. Figure 2.24 illustrates a simplified version of this approach using the example, which compares the VW Passat with the Mercedes C-Class. In moving consumers from consideration to purchase, the VW Passat achieved a conversion rate of only 59 percent; the Mercedes C-Class, in contrast, achieved a rate of 79 percent, some 20 percentage points higher. With the help of the brand potential method it is possible to calculate the contribution of the Mercedes C-Class brand to this higher conversion rate. This calculation shows that if the VW Passat were able to match its brand strength to that of the Mercedes C-Class, it would increase its conversion rate at the purchase stage to just 65 percent. In other words, only 6 percentage points of the total 20-percentage-point gap can potentially be closed through branding. The remaining 14 percentage points of this gap can be attributed to the influence of other elements of the marketing mix.

The analysis reveals a similar situation at the loyalty stage. Here the VW Passat trailed its Mercedes C-Class competitor by an even greater amount, showing a gap of 24 percentage points. However, investing in the brand's development alone can close only 3 percentage points of this gap (see fig. 2.18). Other factors predominate at this stage and include dealership density, resale value, and the perceived price-performance ratio.

Fig. 2.24: The funnel can reveal a brand's potential revenue value (in percent)

	Aided awareness	Familiarity	Consideration	Purchase	Loyalty
VW Passat	52	65	59	39	
Mercedes C-Class	39	50	79	63	
Gap Percentage points	–	–	20	24	
Can be closed by the brand Percentage points	–	–	6	3	
Brand potential (revenue value) EUR millions	–	–	466	115	

Source: McKinsey Brand Health Survey, MCM/McKinsey

The brand purchase funnel reveals how many customers can potentially be retained from stage to stage through improved brand management–but it does not reveal how this will translate into a concrete impact on sales. To establish this, the McKinsey/MCM brand potential method features a special assessment model. In this model, the total acquisition value of the additional customers that can be acquired is a combination of the purchase stage in the brand funnel and the additional value at the loyalty stage. In the VW Passat example, the model theoretically identifies a brand potential of EUR 466 million at the customer acquisition (purchase) stage, with an additional EUR 115 million at the customer retention (loyalty) stage.

Purchase funnel analysis, in combination with the brand potential method, is thus an effective technique for deriving concrete, strategic brand targets and then quantifying and prioritizing them. This enables brand management to become more efficient by focusing on the aspects of the brand that are of especially great potential. Of course, the final decision about where to act first in the purchase funnel will still depend on management's assessment of the organizational capabilities of the company (we will discuss this further in chapter 4). When making such decisions, it is also important to take into account the potential responses of competitors to the intended brand-building activity. Last but not least, the selection of the appropriate benchmark is critical to deriving the right conclusions. What the correct benchmark is will depend on the specific market situation, as well as on the brand's strategic aspirations.

The importance of segment-specific analysis cannot be emphasized sufficiently. It needs to be noted, however, that such analysis is time and context specific. The timeframe in which the potential gains can be captured is limited, depending on the size of the potential and the initial situation specific to the sector and the individual brand; the opportunity is likely to range from two to five years at most.

Notes

1 Sattler, Henrik (ed.), *Praxis von Markenbewertung und Markenmanagement in deutschen Unternehmen*, PwC Deutsche Revision, 2d (Frankfurt: Fachverlag Moderne Wirtschaft, 2001).

2 Extensive primary market studies for both the B2C and the B2B sectors was carried out in conjunction with the renowned market research institute, Marketing Centrum Münster (MCM) at the University of Münster, Germany. The research was directed by Professors Backhaus and Meffert.

3 Representativeness refers to the distribution of age and gender in the population.

4 To allow a meaningful comparison, the ratings were transferred into a standardized scale so that differences between countries become more obvious.

5 Hofstede, Geert, »Culture's Consequences: Comparing Values, Behaviors, Institutions, and Organizations Across Nations,« 2d (Thousand Oaks, CA: Sage Publications, 2003).

6 Caspar, Mirko, Achim Hecker, and Tatjana Sabel, »Markenrelevanz in der Unternehmensführung: Messung, Erklärung und empirische Befunde für B2B-Märkte,« *Arbeitspapier Nr. 4*, ed. Klaus Backhaus et al. (Düsseldorf: publisher, 2002). A total of 48 product markets were surveyed, of which 45 fulfilled the necessary requirements for validity.

7 Cf. de Chernatony, Leslie and Malcolm McDonald, *Creating Powerful Brands in Consumer Services and Industrial Markets* (Oxford: Butterworth-Heinemann, 1998).

8 This is neither a debate about the merits and disadvantages of market segmentation nor a scientific discussion of the methods and techniques of determining target groups. The current market science literature provides comprehensive answers to nearly all these questions (e.g., Bonoma/Shapiro 1984, Meffert 2000).

9 Perrey, Jesko and Ansgar Hölscher, »Nutzenorientierte Kundensegmentierung: Eine Zwischenbilanz nach 35 Jahren,« *Thexis 20*, no. 4 (2004): pp. 8–11.

10 Bonoma, Thomas V. and Benson P. Shapiro, »Evaluating Market Segmentation Approaches,« *Industrial Marketing Management* 13 (1984): pp. 257–268.

11 Perrey, Jesko, *Nutzenorientierte Marktsegmentierung: Ein integrativer Ansatz zum Zielgruppenmarketing im Verkehrsdienstleistungsbereich* (Wiesbaden: Gabler, 1999): p. 129.

12 Voeth, Markus. *Nutzenmessung in der Kaufverhaltensforschung: Die Hierarchisch Individualisierte Limit Conjoint-Analyse (HILCA)* (Wiesbaden: Deutscher Universitätsverlag, 2000).

13 »Publishing the Limit: Capital One Financial Leads a Marketing Revolution,« *Richmond Times-Dispatch*, 26. July 1999, p. 16.

14 Caspar, Mirko and Patrick Metzler, »Entscheidungsorientierte Markenführung: Aufbau und Führung starker Marken,« in: *Arbeitspapier Nr. 3*, ed: Klaus Backhaus et al. (Düsseldorf: publisher, 2002).

15 For instance, the consumer behavior research group of the late Professor Kroeber-Riel; see also: Esch, Franz-Rudolf, *Ein verhaltenswissenschaftlicher Ansatz für die Werbung* (Wiesbaden: Gabler, 1996).

16 See, for example, Low, George S. and Charles W. Lamb Jr., »The measurement and dimensionality of brand associations,« *Journal of Product & Brand Management*, title 8, no 6 (2000): pp. 350–368; Meffert/Burmann, »Identitätsorientierte Markenführung,« 1996.

17 See for instance both the conceptualization of Keller, Kevin L., »Conceptualizing, Measuring, and Managing Customer-Based Brand Equity,« *Journal of Marketing 57* (January 1993): pp. 1–22, and Aaker, David A., *Building Strong Brands* (New York: The Free Press, 1996).

18 Figures according to Euromonitor 2003 for the year 2002.

19 This example from the automobile industry, as well as those described subsequently in this book, are based on an outside-in analysis that McKinsey carried out as part of an international benchmark initiative in more than twenty product markets. The examples do not use any confidential data gathered within the framework of client relationships.

3.
Making Brands

Brands are mostly made, not born. They do not arise accidentally; their growth and development can be measured and predicted. This is the main message of this book.

The success of a brand is measurable at every stage along its path: tools and instruments exist that can measure the status of a brand in the competitive environment. We have already introduced four of these tools in chapter 2:

- The tachometer of brand relevance: determines how relevant brands are in influencing purchasing decisions in a particular market.
- Market segmentation: identifies, evaluates, and defines a brand's target customer groups.
- The brand diamond: analyzes the various components of the brand image, tangible and intangible, and rational and emotional elements.
- The brand purchase funnel: segments and compares customer recognition, affinity, and commitment to a brand at the various stages that lead to purchase.

Brand managers need to be familiar with these analytical methods and know how to apply them. They reveal the facts of the matter, but they do not tell you what to do to strengthen the brand. Therefore, for the brand manager, many questions have yet to be answered. What can be done to restore the luxury brand to its former glory? How can strong brands be protected from the competition and made even stronger? Can the existing product promise be adjusted, or is it necessary to develop a completely new promise? What impact will it have on the organization if we follow advertising agency recommendations and make the brand more emotional? This chapter will begin to answer these important questions.

3.1 Brand Driver Analysis: Deriving Strategic Brand Direction and Initiatives for Growth

The brand purchase funnel measures the performance of the brand at the various stages leading to purchase and loyalty. It reveals where there are gaps in comparison with relevant competitors, quantifies these gaps, and ranks them according to their significance. These facts make transparent where a brand's strengths and weakness exist, but they leave brand management with a serious question: how can these gaps be closed? To be more precise, how can the brand be repositioned relative to competitors so that current and potential customers will better notice it, and how can it capture the untapped sales indicated by the brand potential analysis? Looking back at the examples discussed in earlier chapters, brand managers need to understand what factors are responsible for shortcomings along the purchase funnel.

- What caused the dramatic gap between the VW Passat and the Mercedes C-Class in converting potential customers into buyers?
- Why does Samsung lag behind industry leader Nokia in becoming a consumer's favorite mobile phone manufacturer?
- What drives Camel's gap compared with Marlboro in converting one-time customers into frequent buyers of the brand?
- Why are German tourists less likely to consider Switzerland than Austria as a potential holiday destination?

What is really important for the consumer?

To be able to establish what is really important for the consumer, we need to first identify all the necessary elements of the brand image in order to lead consumers from one stage of the purchase funnel to the next. We refer to these critical brand elements as *brand drivers*. Comparing one's own brand drivers with those of competitors yields a profile of strengths and weaknesses. Brand drivers and their respective strengths can then be combined to form a matrix. From this matrix, it is possible to derive what options management has for growing the brand and setting its strategic direction.

The first step is, therefore, to ensure that the brand drivers are correctly identified. To ensure that this is done, all the potential drivers, as well as the current ones, must be taken into consideration. It is best practice to structure each individual driver using the brand diamond (as described in section 2.2). Figure 3.1 shows a template of the potential drivers of brand image used as the starting point for a broad analysis of brand drivers in the high street retail trade.

These associations are based on surveys of consumer focus groups and discussions with market experts. The brand associations elicited from

Fig. 3.1: Brand diamond analysis of a retail chain

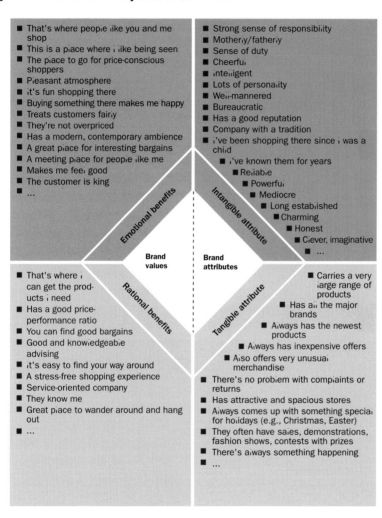

Source: McKinsey

tangible attributes essentially describe operational levers, such as the quality of product assortment (»always has the newest products«), the layout of the sales floor (»has attractive and spacious stores«), or distribution (»has a good location«). The other fields of the brand diamond comprise associations that reflect the perceived customer benefit or intangible brand attributes.

This analysis produces a complete map of brand elements, analogous to fig. 3.1. This is the starting point for brand driver analysis. The next step is to establish how strongly the individual elements of the brand diamond are linked to the brand and which associations are responsible for the actual performance of the brand in the purchase process. The results indicate which brand elements best account for customer conversion at each stage in the purchase funnel.

Numerous methods of market research are available to analyze the behavioral relevance of the brand elements. A simple method frequently used is the direct customer survey of the most important attributes. It is important to note that the results of such surveys can be misleading, however. The fact that all consumers would like the best possible performance for the least possible money actually tells you very little. Market researchers refer to this as *expectation inflation*.

A better method is to determine consumers' actual priorities indirectly using analytical methods. Although a range of multivariate techniques can be used to achieve this, the most common technique is to compare the average values. The average values of all brand elements are compared at two sequential stages of the purchase funnel. Those brand elements that show the greatest improvement in the average values from one stage to the next are the main brand drivers. In contrast, brand elements whose average values do not change in the transition from one stage to the next are not significant for that step in the purchase funnel. A good example of what this means in practice is the attribute of airline safety. The mean values of this attribute will not differ at the purchase and loyalty stages. This is because the safety of major airlines is likely to be considered equally important by both one-time users and loyal customers. The situation might be very different, however, for an attribute such as punctuality. The punctuality (or lack thereof) of an airline might well be of great significance in encouraging (or discouraging) the transition from being a one-time customer to that of becoming a loyal customer.

As shown in fig. 3.2, using the example of brand driver analysis carried out by McKinsey in the automobile market, the priorities that consumers cite directly often differ considerably from those derived analytically, rein-

Fig. 3.2: What customers say they want when they buy a car, and what they really value

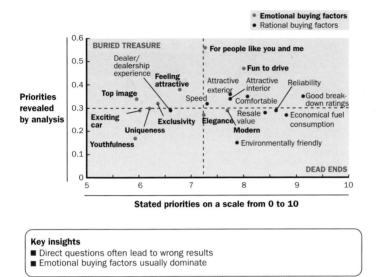

- Emotional buying factors
- Rational buying factors

Priorities revealed by analysis

BURIED TREASURE

For people like you and me

Dealer/dealership experience

Feeling attractive

Fun to drive

Attractive exterior

Attractive interior

Reliability

Top image

Speed

Comfortable

Good break-down ratings

Exciting car

Exclusivity

Elegance

Resale value

Economical fuel consumption

Uniqueness

Modern

Youthfulness

Environmentally friendly

DEAD ENDS

Stated priorities on a scale from 0 to 10

Key insights
- Direct questions often lead to wrong results
- Emotional buying factors usually dominate

Source: McKinsey Brand Health Survey, MCM/McKinsey

forcing the point that brand managers need to be cautious when using direct measurement methods if they are not to find themselves skating on thin ice. The reality is that people do not always do what they say they will. This discrepancy becomes particularly obvious when looking at environmental issues, for example. In direct surveys in the mid-size automobile market, many consumers claim to place great value on environmental protection. This is not that surprising; after all, who would say openly that they choose to be environmentally destructive? But when this statement is tested, environmental considerations do not turn out to be truly relevant as a brand driver in purchasing a car. In consequence, it is not surprising that Europe's new generation of revolutionary, ultra fuel-efficient (78 miles per gallon) cars have not been as successful as was expected. Despite what people might claim in surveys, fuel-guzzling SUVs continue to hog the roads.

An analysis of consumer priorities needs to be performed for each stage of the purchase funnel. Once complete, this analysis will paint a clear picture of the consumer's path through each subsequent stage of the purchase funnel. Figure 3.3 shows the results of this type of analysis using the automobile example. This illustration shows that the VW Passat had a high

Fig. 3.3: When buying a car, emotional values are in the driver's seat

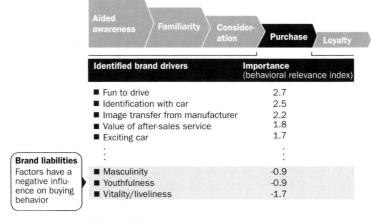

Identified brand drivers	Importance (behavioral relevance index)
■ Fun to drive	2.7
■ Identification with car	2.5
■ Image transfer from manufacturer	2.2
■ Value of after-sales service	1.8
■ Exciting car	1.7
⋮	⋮
■ Masculinity	-0.9
■ Youthfulness	-0.9
■ Vitality/liveliness	-1.7

Brand liabilities
Factors have a negative influence on buying behavior

Source: McKinsey Brand Health Survey, MCM/McKinsey

potential for capturing sales relative to its competitor, the Mercedes C-Class, especially in the transition from consideration to purchase. The analysis shows that the brand driver »fun to drive« had the strongest influence on consumer behavior. The next four brand elements are all of similar relevance to each other in influencing the purchase decision but are much less important than being »fun to drive.«

The relative importance of the brand drivers is determined by the behavioral relevance index. According to this ranking, the element »vitality« is a brand liability. It has a negative influence on purchasing behavior and prevents a better conversion rate to the purchase stage. Just as positive brand drivers improve brand performance in the purchase process, negative ones adversely influence the mind of consumers. Although it might not be intuitively obvious, the analysis shows that an overly »vital« or »lively« image for the VW Passat would have had a negative impact on sales in its vehicle class.

Once the brand drivers have been determined, the next step is to carry out an analysis of the strengths and weaknesses of the brand. Quite simply, in this analysis, the attributes of a company's brand are compared to those of the market average and the most important competitors, taking into consideration all the brand drivers prioritized for each stage of the brand funnel. This reveals where a company's brand has been able to establish a strong, differentiated position and in which brand drivers it lags behind the competition. Figure 3.4 illustrates the strengths and weaknesses analysis in

Making Brands

Fig. 3.4: VW Passat and Mercedes C-Class: Comparison of strengths and weaknesses (difference in percent)

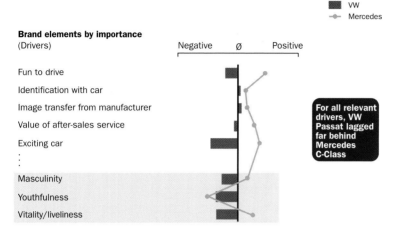

VW
Mercedes

Brand elements by importance
(Drivers)

Negative   Ø   Positive

Fun to drive

Identification with car

Image transfer from manufacturer

Value of after-sales service

Exciting car

Masculinity

Youthfulness

Vitality/liveliness

For all relevant drivers, VW Passat lagged far behind Mercedes C-Class

Source: McKinsey Brand Health Survey, MCM/McKinsey

the automotive market. The excerpt shown in the example clearly demonstrates that the VW Passat not only performed worse than its competitor in the two relevant brand elements »fun to drive« and »exciting car,« but it also lagged behind the market average.

Defining the options for action

In order to define the potential options management has for influencing the brand, the analyses of brand drivers and strengths and weaknesses are combined to produce a matrix of options for action. This matrix will highlight key issues for management:

- If a company's brand shows weaknesses in key brand elements, these are potential starting points for improving the brand image. Strongly negative brand elements need to be addressed immediately; these must be eliminated or at least minimized in order to improve the brand's performance in the purchase process.
- Conversely, if the brand demonstrates strengths in important elements, these should be maintained or expanded further. Less important brand elements that are particularly strong may also help to differentiate the

brand; however, it needs to be remembered that they have only an indirect impact on purchasing behavior.

Figure 3.5 shows an example of this type of actionable matrix of options for the VW Passat. Here, the »fun to drive« brand driver possesses a high degree of relevance in the purchase process. However, it is significantly weaker for the VW Passat than for the competition. It thus represents a potential starting point for optimizing the brand image. The matrix answers the question of why the VW Passat lagged so far behind the Mercedes C-Class in 2002 when it came to converting potential customers into buyers: in the relevant emotional brand drivers, the VW Passat appeared to be more weakly perceived than the competition. This is the point where management needed to intervene.

We will now revisit the case studies mentioned earlier to examine the options for optimizing the brand image.

Mobile phones: Outside-in analysis of the purchase funnel in summer 2006 indicates that Samsung still lags behind its competitor Nokia in becoming a consumer's favorite choice (see fig. 2.21). The brand driver analysis shows that characteristics of prime importance to increase conversion rates in this case are »easy to use,« »a brand you can trust,« »good quality,« and »a brand you are happy to be seen using« (see fig. 3.6).

Fig. 3.5: The VW Passat needed to build emotional brand drivers in order to improve its performance in the buying process

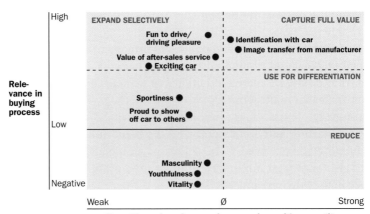

Strengths and weaknesses in comparison with competitors

Source: McKinsey Brand Health Survey, MCM/McKinsey

Making Brands

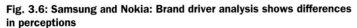

Fig. 3.6: Samsung and Nokia: Brand driver analysis shows differences in perceptions

Deviations from market average in percent

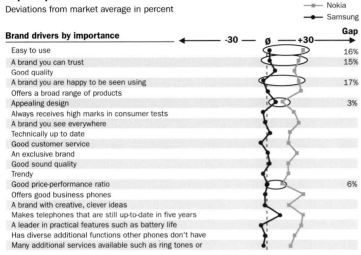

Source: McKinsey German consumer survey, 2006

The strengths and weaknesses profiles of Nokia and Samsung show that Nokia is assessed significantly more positively than Samsung overall. The profile also reveals that the Samsung brand achieves very similar ratings to Nokia's on attributes like »appealing design« and »global price-performance ratio.« However, as has been mentioned, these are not the main drivers that determined consumer's choice of their favorite mobile phone brand.

When this information is transferred to a matrix of options for action, it is clear that Samsung has its work cut out for it (see fig. 3.7). Samsung will not be able to significantly close the gap to Nokia purely by emphasizing its strenghts of modernity, quality and design, as these brand elements are of medium to low importance to consumers. To increase funnel performance, Samsung must improve on the convenience aspect (»easy-to-use«) as well as the emotional benefits of trust and reputation (»happy to be seen with«).

The Samsung management is trying to increase its emphasis on emotional brand features. By launching its new »Imagine« campaign to replace the ubiquitous »DigitAll Everyone's invited« in 2005, as well as recruiting brand spokespersons like Chelsea football coach Jose Mourinho, the brand is clearly trying to build trust and improve on the »show off«-factor.[1]

Fig. 3.7: "Easy to use" is the most important improvement point

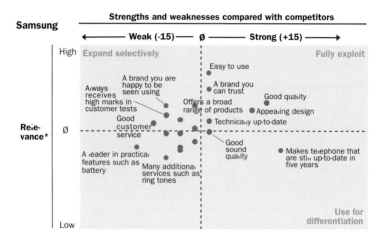

* Brand driver values are derived from the Consideration to Favorite stages of the funnel
Source: McKinsey German consumer survey, 2006

Tobacco: As the matrix of options for actions in fig. 3.8 shows, Camel is perceived as weaker than Marlboro in nearly all relevant drivers in the Spanish cigarette market. To build the brand, Camel needs to develop further key drivers in addition to its few existing functional strengths (its smooth taste and quality/price relationship). Emotional benefits are highly relevant in this market, including, for instance, »makes me feel good,« »brand you trust,« and »for people like you and me.« Developing these would help Camel close the gap with Marlboro by converting one-time customers to frequent buyers.

Tourism: In the analysis comparing Switzerland and Austria as tourist destinations, Switzerland trailed Austria as a possible destination at the brand funnel stage »consideration.« A segment-specific evaluation shows that Switzerland's brand image (and the concomitant brand drivers) differs considerably across segments, depending on the age group of the potential tourists. For those under the age of 40, the most important criteria when it comes to considering a vacation destination are a »trendy destination« and »charming.« For the segment over the age of 40, the most important drivers are »good value for money« and »high quality« (see fig. 3.9). The segment-specific analysis also shows that Switzerland's image is far more negative among younger people than older ones. To appeal to the

Fig. 3.8: Matrix of options for action for Came! re:ative to Mar:boro

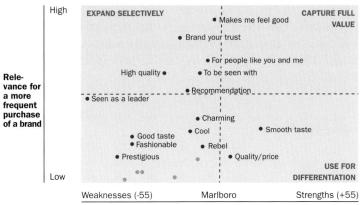

Strengths and weaknesses of Camel vs. Marlboro

Source: McKinsey Spanish market research, April 2005 (n = 501)

Fig. 3.9: Switzerland's image problem in tourism: "high-priced" and "old-fashioned" (in percent)

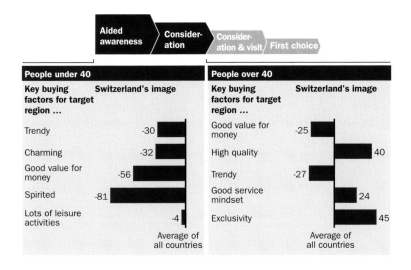

Source: McKinsey survey, conducted in Germany

younger age group, Switzerland will need to rejuvenate its image. For the older target group, it should emphasize the perception that it has value for money.

This example of the use of brand driver analysis in tourism clearly demonstrates that the brand purchase funnel is most effective when the various purchasing stages are segmented and considered target-group by target-group. This segmentation requires that appropriate benchmarks are chosen for each stage in the brand purchase funnel.

Selecting benchmarks

In order to apply brand driver analysis effectively, it is necessary to assess each respective stage of the purchase funnel separately and to select appropriate benchmarks for each stage.

Take into account the stage of the purchase funnel: The individual brand drivers do not possess the same relevance at all stages of the purchase funnel. Price, for instance, is very important at the transition from consideration to purchase. In establishing customer loyalty, however, price plays only a secondary role in many sectors; dimensions of emotional benefit are much more important at this stage, as demonstrated in the mobile phone example.

A matrix of options for action can, of course, be generated for each stage of the purchase funnel, but the matrix that addresses the stage with the highest potential for improvement is always of special interest for a brand. If no single stage stands out in the purchase funnel analysis, it makes sense to generate an aggregate matrix of options for action. This enables all the main drivers of all the stages in the purchase funnel to be examined together.

Choosing the right benchmarks: In the matrix of options for action, the strengths and weaknesses of a brand are always assessed in relation to those of a benchmark brand. This benchmark is usually either a single competitor or an industry average. In selecting a benchmark, one should orient oneself toward the current position of a company's brand and its strategic level of aspiration. For a relatively new brand, for instance, selecting the market leader as the sole benchmark is unlikely to identify anything other than significant weaknesses in the matrix of options for action. This wouldn't be very helpful, as it would make it very nearly impossible to choose a meaningful strategic option for building the brand. Instead, by considering a more conservative benchmark, in this case, for instance, the market average, more useful results can be developed.

Changing direction

Brand driver analysis allows management to determine the strategic direction of the brand using the matrix of options for action. Orienting the brand strategy toward selected brand drivers will lead to improved brand performance at the respective stages of the purchase funnel. The unanswered question here is whether or not the competitors' brand strategy should also be taken into account.

It is a fundamental principle of brand management that a brand must not only be better than those of its competitors, but also distinctive from them. If all brands relied on the same brand drivers (simply because they are relevant) they would be interchangeable from the consumer's perspective. In other words, market differentiation would disappear, commoditizing the brand. To avoid this, it is important to examine whether a selected strategic direction potentially leads to:

- The brand assuming a position already held by another competing brand (in single-brand decisions); or
- The brand being oriented in such a way that it will conflict with another of the company's own brands (in multiple-brand decisions).

Of course, in certain cases, it may be in management's interest to attack the position of a competitor by repositioning a brand. Typically, however, sustainable brand building will aim towards differentiation from the competition.

This challenge often proves difficult in multiple-brand strategies. Management of brand portfolios attempts, typically, to optimize positioning in the overall market through the selective positioning of single brands.[2] In a group of companies with several brands, however, single brands will often be repositioned without considering the consequences for the overall portfolio. In such circumstances, making the right decisions about prioritization while also balancing all the costs and profit effects presents a major challenge. Section 3.3 will specifically cover this problem and how the BrandMatics® approach can help deal with it in a systematic manner.

Brand Management in the Linde Group of Companies

by Hubertus Krossa, member of the executive board, Linde AG, responsible for material handling

The Linde brand – A »LeadIng« proposition

In 1879, scientist Carl von Linde founded the »Gesellschaft für Lindes Eismaschinen AG« in Wiesbaden, laying the foundation for this international group of high-tech companies. The Linde brand aspires to continuously expand its leading international position in the business divisions of Gas and Engineering, and Material Handling through commitment to innovation and comprehensive expertise. The company focuses especially on providing complete solutions in order to better understand and fulfill customer's individual needs.

The company's leading position is based on the values of quality, expertise, and innovation. »Made by Linde» is the anchor of its communication, both internally and externally. Quality, expertise, and innovation are Linde's three overarching brand values that have enabled it to establish itself as the market leader in materials handling. Linde seeks to fulfill the promise of its brand value not only for all its customers, but also for its employees.

The Linde Group has built itself into one of the world's largest manufacturers of industrial trucks, manufacturing three brands, Linde, Still, and OM Pimespo. Linde is one of the few suppliers to offer a complete range of products: engine-powered forklift trucks, electric trucks, and warehouse trucks. With more than 100,000 forklifts and warehouse trucks sold yearly, the Linde Group is the number one supplier in Europe today.

Linde represents a premium brand in the European market for industrial trucks. A European-wide study recently carried out on brand strength and customer satisfaction showed that in the overall market, Linde leads by a large margin in fulfilling the most demanding customer requirements. Alongside the high standard of quality and innovativeness of this long-standing brand, Linde's success is attributable to its professional, well-coordinated dealer structure in all markets. In France and England, the two leading brands Fenwick and Lansing have been successfully integrated into Linde's brand organization.

Still has been a part of Linde's brand portfolio in material handling since 1973. Historically strong in the domain of electric counterbalance forklift trucks, today Still covers the entire product portfolio of industrial trucks in Europe. Its distribution and service structure comprises company-owned branch offices that focus on the complete range of service packages for in-plant logistics, going well beyond the production, delivery, and maintenance of industrial trucks. The assortment of Still products and services ranges from complete, industry-specific solutions to computer-aided logistic programs for effective warehouse management.

OM (Officine Mecchaniche) Pimespo, an Italian brand with a long tradition, was integrated into the Linde Group in 1992. With its slogan »Designed to work,« this brand stands for reliable forklifts and warehouse trucks that give customers outstanding value for money. OM Pimespo has long been the market leader in Italy using this positioning, but OM Pimespo also maintains branch offices in other European markets. With its value-for-money strategy, the brand nicely rounds out the product assortment in the brand portfolio of Linde Material Handling.

Linde's strong commitment to this multiple-brand strategy in the Material Handling division is based on the realization that, in order to maximize success in the overall market, one needs to appeal specifically to different customer needs through separate brands. It is crucial here that the Linde Group assumes a different positioning with each brand so that it can minimize cannibalization and at the same time secure the best possible differentiation with respect to the relevant competition. It is important to understand the precise nature of the brands in order to perform this brand balancing act and to direct it actively in every product segment and in the various local markets.

Linde takes a systematic approach to this task based on a European, country-specific segmentation and a precise analysis of the purchase decision-making process both for Linde brands and the most important competitors. This analysis is carried out in each relevant product category in the most important international markets. Fig. 3.10 shows the results of a purchase funnel analysis that was conducted in 2003. The sample Linde brand selected for the analysis shows a brand awareness of 97 percent, an outstanding figure in this product category. During subsequent process stages, however, the brand successively loses ground in comparison with the best in class. The main weaknesses arise in the transition to the familiarity and purchase stages. At these points in the purchase funnel, the brand significantly lags behind the best in class, with a gap of 23 and 31 percentage points, respectively. Overall, the brand

Fig. 3.10: The Linde brand of forklift trucks needed a major makeover to catch up (in percent)

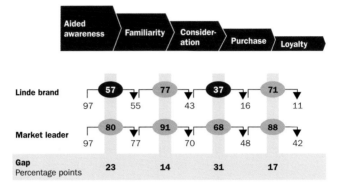

Source: Linde AG, Brand Positioning Team

Fig. 3.11: How familiarity with a forklift truck brand arises (in percent)

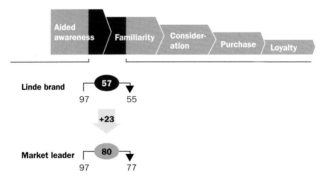

Prioritized brand drivers	Importance (behavioral relevance index)
■ Ergonomics and user-friendliness	10.0
■ A brand you can recommend	9.8
■ Rapid problem solving	8.0
■ More than just a product	7.0
■ Reliably engineered	7.0
■ Long-standing tradition	6.9
■ Qualified salespeople	6.8

Relevant product attributes
■ Ergonomic operating elements
■ Good suspension supporting driver's work area/cab
■ Roomy cab
■ Versatility in handling/transporting different types of loads

Source: Linde AG, Brand Positioning Team

is able to convert only 11 percent of those surveyed into loyal customers (which, incidentally, provides further evidence of the usefulness of a multiple-brand strategy).

Starting with the purchase funnel analysis, the reasons for the existing weaknesses of brands in the Linde Group can now be analyzed. It is, of course, important to know what brand elements are responsible in particular for the transition from one stage of the purchase funnel to the next. Fig. 3.11 shows the results of this type of analysis for the transition from the »awareness« stage to that of »familiarity.« The analysis in the specific product segments shows that a combination of emotional and rational attributes is especially important here. In order to derive targeted actions, the respective brand elements can also be subdivided into more detailed and concrete product attributes. It turns out that ergonomic operating elements, good suspension of the operator's work area/cab and a spacious operator's cab are responsible for the perception overall of ergonomics and user-friendliness.

From the results of the brand driver analysis, together with a strengths and weaknesses analysis, Linde is then in a position to derive the range of actions for brand optimization and to represent these in a matrix (see fig. 3.12). This representation makes it possible to derive a clear indication of how to improve current brand positioning. The example shows that in the product segment under consideration, the Linde brand analyzed has weaknesses in the important drivers of »ergonomics« and »a brand you can recommend.« Potential for improvement also exists in the attribute »rapid problem solving.« In contrast, the brand's good price positioning should be maintained due to its strong differentiation.

This brief example illuminates the systematic approach Linde implemented in the course of optimizing and improving its multi-brand strategy. In addition to deriving short-range measures to improve the presence of every individual brand, the analysis and data acquired are also used to improve strategic brand positioning. It is, after all, very important that marketing decisions flow directly into product development. Besides taking advantage of existing synergies, Linde plans to pool technical expertise as well as to increase significantly the share of the group's components used in the products, while at the same time being careful to ensure that the use of common parts never leads to products appearing the same from the customer's perspective.

For Linde, brand management is a top priority; decisions about brand portfolios are made at corporate headquarters. The independent imple-

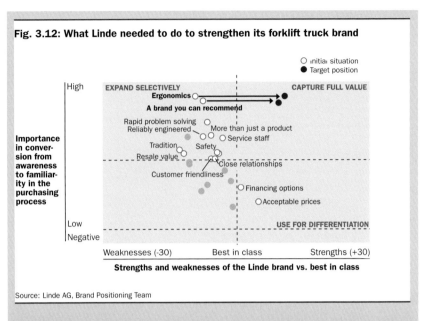

Fig. 3.12: What Linde needed to do to strengthen its forklift truck brand

○ initial situation
● Target position

High — EXPAND SELECTIVELY — CAPTURE FULL VALUE

Ergonomics

A brand you can recommend

Rapid problem solving

Reliably engineered

More than just a product

Service staff

Tradition

Safety

Resale value

Close relationships

Customer friendliness

Financing options

Acceptable prices

Importance in conversion from awareness to familiarity in the purchasing process

Low

Negative

USE FOR DIFFERENTIATION

Weaknesses (-30)   Best in class   Strengths (+30)

Strengths and weaknesses of the Linde brand vs. best in class

Source: Linde AG, Brand Positioning Team

mentation of these decisions in product development, distribution, andmarketing strategies through the individual company brands is actively monitored and the results are reviewed on an ongoing basis. In this process, the corporate marketing department directs the development and implementation of strategies and marketing plans. The development of actions takes place in an ongoing dialogue between corporate headquarters, brand organization, and local subsidiaries. The corporate marketing department must mediate between the brand organizations in a neutral and objective manner. Although it is important to avoid internal cannibalization, internal competition can be useful in the search for better ideas. In this manner the Linde Group ensures that it achieves its aspiration of superior innovativeness, both now and in the future. »LeadIng« (see my text in chapter text later) has been the motto at Linde since 1879, and will remain so in the future.

3.2 Pathways Analysis: Defining and Synthesizing the Brand Promise and Putting it into Operation

Brand driver analysis and the matrix of options for action provide answers to the questions about which brand elements drive the purchasing process, which are the best options in terms of positioning, and what effect these options will have on the competitive environment.

But brand building is more than merely specifying strategic direction. This direction must also be synthesized into an overall concept and then translated into operational terms, so that all employees are aware of exactly what individual contributions they can make in implementing the strategy so as to craft a strong brand. Due to their complexity, these tasks of making the brand strategy concrete and of putting it into operation frequently appear to be major stumbling blocks even for the best brand strategy.

- *Defining the brand promise:* The brand promise takes into account the analysis of the brand and the strategic considerations. It describes both the essence of the brand and its differentiation with respect to current and potential customers, as well as within the company's own portfolio. Ideally, this promise culminates in a concise phrase or brand vision, even if this conciseness comes somewhat at the cost of the various individual elements.
- *Putting the brand promise into operation:* Even the most clever brand promise will fall short if it is not embedded in the organization. The goal is to ensure that the brand promise is communicated to and understood by all the relevant employees and corporate units. It is only possible to implement a brand promise that is defined clearly so that it is connected to concrete actions, for instance, in terms of the service and product design.

When the brand promise has been made concrete and put into action, a brand vision should emerge. This will consist, typically, of a short slogan or phrase that will be used in external communication of the brand. This serves as a point of reference both internally and externally. The brand vision should always form the framework for all strategic and operational tasks of brand management regardless of whether these involve developing a product concept, planning a product exhibition, optimizing a set of product components, or conducting a direct marketing campaign.

Skoda automobiles can be used as an example to illustrate this process. Its brand vision, developed jointly with Volkswagen Group marketing in 1998, relies on the brand promise: »Solid quality based on more than 100 years tradition at reasonable prices.« This is put into operation, among other means, by using a »traditional and functional oriented image« that emphasizes rational benefits in its communication. Though Skoda's campaigns might not win prizes for their creativity, they nonetheless clearly appeal to its target group, as confirmed by Skoda's increased sales.

The brand vision does not appear like a bolt of lightning from the blue, however. It is derived through a step-by-step process.

Concentrating on the essentials

Summarizing the brand promise in a brand vision statement is one of the most challenging tasks for management. Even if all the analyses described in section 3.1 are available, it is not easy to distill their essence. This is all the more challenging, as the brand vision needs to include, in a concise yet complete manner, all the factors that are essential in differentiating the brand.

The point from which to start is to ask what the brand represents from the consumer's point of view. In answering this question, agencies and consultants often offer seemingly endless lists of visions, missions, values, emotional and rational attributes, core beliefs, supportive beliefs, personalities, identities, etc. In other words, they are not sufficiently based on facts.

A certain retailer, for instance, defined its brand promise using fifteen brand values, from »inspiration« to »ingenuity,« »fun,« »self-confidence,« and »trust« to »good value for money.« Nothing was left out. With this degree of fuzziness, the retailer could represent all conceivable formats, from Giorgio Armani to H&M or Gap. Additionally, it addressed nearly all conceivable dimensions of value. Who wouldn't want to shop there? When one of the authors of this book read aloud another colorful medley of positioning attributes, such as »friendly,« »honest,« and »helpful,« to his partner, her guess as to the identity of the brand was, »It must be a church!« A reasonable guess under the circumstances.

Another example is a service provider that not only compiled a long list of general statements about its brand promise, but also went so far as to arrange them into a number of categories: from »value proposition« and »core values« to »inner-directed values,« »outer-directed values,« and »personality traits.« The brand promise seemed to be trying to answer questions that no one was asking. To cap it all, the service provider exceeded one hundred words in defining who its target customers were.

Establishing a successful brand promise is by no means child's play as it involves expert craftsmanship. Once complete it will define, for all those working with the brand, the brand's benefits for its customers (the brand promise) and will be encapsulated in a few short phrases as the basis for all marketing communication.

Once the brand driver analysis has revealed the brand elements that support a company's own competitive position, the task is then to derive the correct brand promise from this set of conceivable elements, identify its core areas of differentiation, review them on an ongoing basis, and update them as needed. Unfortunately there is no patented formula for which elements can be combined and in what manner to derive the brand promise; however, a checklist of guidelines does exist (see fig. 3.13).

- *Distinctiveness:* Concentrate on strong and distinctive brand elements (derived from the matrix of options for action; see section 3.1).
- *Relevance:* Take into consideration the important brand elements in the customer's purchasing/selection decision (again, taken from the options for action).
- *Credibility:* Ensure that the brand promise is credible (it is unconvincing, for instance, to place special emphasis on the dimension of price for high-end shops).
- *Consistency:* Maintain consistency with past brand presence and brand heritage (see chapter 2 for examples of inconsistency in brand presence).
- *Feasibility:* Secure internal performance capabilities. The company needs to possess the internal resources and capabilities necessary for ensuring that the brand promise can be fulfilled consistently in all its contacts with customers. It is especially important to take into consideration the costs of implementing the brand promise.

Fig. 3.13: Checklist for deriving the brand promise

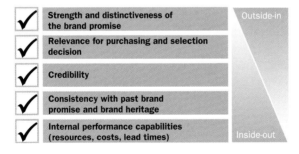

Source: McKinsey

The Matrix of Options for Action

Which brand elements get priority; the most relevant or the strongest?

Brand managers are often faced with making fundamental decisions based on the assessment of the matrix of options for action. Often this presents them with a dilemma: which of the two dimensions in the matrix »strength« or »relevance« (fig. 3.14) should be given preference? Should a company's own strengths, and thus its differentiation from competitors, be expanded first, even if the importance of these elements is relatively low? Or would it be better to eliminate existing weaknesses in important elements crucial to purchasing decisions?

Unfortunately, there is no universal answer to this question; a case-by-case approach is necessary. However, it is indisputable that any weaknesses in important »hygiene factors« for the rational elements of the brand need to be eliminated first. This means, for instance, that airlines must be safe, taxi services on time, and personal care products gentle on the skin. If the next step involves further selection of brand-defining elements, a prioritization based on the checklist in figure 3.14 is necessary.

In making such decisions, the company needs always to weigh market requirements (the outside-in perspective or market-based view) against its own resources (the inside-out perspective or resource-based view). When taking an inside-out perspective, as well as considering financial resources and timing, staff and management capabilities and know-how also need to be taken into account. The best theoretical brand promise is useless if it would take too long to deliver it effectively or if the company lacks the capabilities and resources to carry it out.

Often a compromise will need to be made, therefore, between a purely market-based approach and one that takes a more pragmatic line with the resources required to execute this. In other words, »strengthening your strengths« should take priority over »eliminating your weaknesses.« In this manner one can ensure that the brand remains unique and can retain its distinct profile in the competitive environment.[3]

Be careful, however. A brand's identity is worthless if the attributes that it conveys are perceived by customers to be of no interest, because they are not important for them today, nor likely to be so in the future. Managing a brand along its identity, an approach outlined in numerous textbooks, does not free the brand manager from the responsibility for analyzing and improving the company's brand image in terms of the

Fig. 3.14: Strengthen strengths or reduce weaknesses?
Case-by-case decision

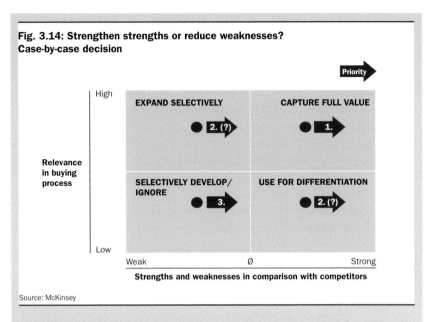

Source: McKinsey

outside-in customer perspective. Regardless of how meticulous and cautious one is in further developing brand identity, the best resources of a brand, whether tangible or intangible, are of no use if they don't generate relevant associations among (potential) customers. A long-established retailer, for instance, might rely on its tradition all it wants, but if this image is associated with out-of-date aspects, it will fail. In other words, following a purely inside-out approach by focusing mainly on the brand's heritage and key strengths is not a recipe for success *sine qua non*, either.

Focusing exclusively on overcoming a brand's weaknesses is also a poor approach in most cases because it is likely to lead to »me too« decisions. In the worst case, the company never gets off the treadmill of trying to catch up. Focusing too much on weak points can lead a company to invest in brand elements or positions that are already better covered by competitors' strong brands. Since these competitors will likely be striving to improve their strengths, this is very shaky ground on which to build.

To sum up, in order to define the »right« brand promise, brand management needs to analyze and evaluate the market perspective, including the brand's current strengths and weaknesses, as well as the company's internal perspective with respect to its resources and capabilities.

The criteria included in the checklist above will form the basis for assessing and prioritizing the brand elements. For this purpose, the criteria are transformed into a simple scoring model. As with all scoring models, the key question is how to weight the criteria. Their weighting in the checklist should be oriented first and foremost towards the initial situation of the brand and the associated strategy. In a stable environment (e.g., in the case of market leaders such as BMW, Persil, or Nivea), the criteria of consistency and ensuring their internal performance are certainly of highest importance. Typically in such cases, this exercise would not produce an entirely new brand promise but would update and improve the existing one (see fig. 3.15).

Once this exercise is complete, the brand promise can now be summarized and shaped into the brand vision for external use. Figure 3.16 demonstrates this concept using the example of the Skoda vision statement from 1998.

Fig. 3.15: New profile for BMW

"The Essence of the Brand: Joy"

BMW, Mini, Rolls-Royce: the three makes couldn't be more different. Thanks to an ingeniously designed and executed branding strategy, they each have personality characteristics that distinguish them for customers and against competitors.

The saying has been around for 25 years. It graces every advertisement and can be heard in every radio and TV spot. "BMW – Freude am Fahren." Or in English: "BMW – the ultimate driving machine." For Executive Board chairman Helmut Panke, that's what BMW stands for in the eyes of customers: "joy" as the brand essence, "dynamic" as the key brand value. Why does it matter? "The core is the heart or the essence of a brand, the ultimate customer value," says a BMW company report. "The values and their distinctive facets are the personality traits that collectively and uniquely stand for a brand."

In the past, BMW sought to associate its brand exclusively with "dynamic" and appeal primarily to career-minded go-getters on their way up. Now, because "one-dimensional positioning" jeopardizes the brand's success in the long term, the board has augmented it with the new elements "challenging" and "cultivated." As the Group's brand manifesto confidently announces: "To enable BMW to appeal to new target groups, we will position ourselves using all three brands." The Mini stands for "enthusiasm," its values are "chic, integrative, and extroverted."

As a result, the brand is said to have "a strong emotional appeal without being polarizing." It does not want to be a traditional automotive status symbol. Instead, its appeal is inclusiveness, "linking classes, peoples, countries, the young and the old."

Rolls-Royce is the "ultimate luxury brand." The car of choice for the super-rich conveys "presence," its values are "grace, endurance, and ambition." It is "admired and respected, it radiates majesty, charisma, and style and makes a clear statement – for itself and its owner."

Source: "Freude als Markenkern", *Capital*, 19 Sept. 2002, p 45 (translation)

Making Brands

Fig. 3.16: The Skoda 1998 brand vision

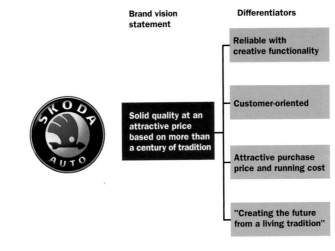

Source: Volkswagen AG, 1998

The Skoda brand vision was developed as part of a comprehensive process by which the Volkswagen group has developed a multiple-brand strategy. After acquiring Seat in 1986 and Skoda in 1990, the Volkswagen group was faced with a difficult task. On the one hand, the individual brands in the brand portfolio (including Volkswagen and Audi) needed to be positioned as leaders in as many attractive automobile segments as possible, but without competing with one another. On the other hand, it was important that the group capture the cost synergies resulting from their integrated platform strategy. In this context, it was very important that the platform cost synergies should have no impact on the brand differentiation. These two aspects are, therefore, managed separately, so the customers remain unaware of the group's platform synergies.

The new brand visions for the entire group's corporate brands were created in 1998 in a joint development process headed by the corporate marketing department. Whereas Volkswagen is the universal brand of the »strong middle« (the mid-priced market that resides between economy cars and luxury models), Audi is the premium brand with a sporty, emotional orientation. In the more price-sensitive automobile segments, the Skoda brand is designed to appeal to the more functionally oriented buyers, whereas Seat is designed to have more of an emotional appeal.

The fundamental principles of Skoda's 1998 brand vision statement are still valid today; it has nevertheless been refined continuously over the years. As mentioned, the element »Solid quality based on more than 100 years of tradition at reasonable prices« was selected as the core (or the essence) of the brand. This brand essence was promoted through four differentiators or brand values: »reliable with innovative functionality,« »customer oriented,« »attractive purchase and running costs,« and »future from tradition.« Considering Skoda's brand presence at the time, this brand vision certainly underlined the visionary aspiration of the Volkswagen Group and of Skoda in seeking to position the Eastern European brand in the functionality-oriented lower-price segment. In 2005 Skoda was able to increase the number of cars it sold by more than 10 percent compared with 2004. Though Volkswagen AG has faced a number of other problems in recent years, Skoda's success has confirmed the overall soundness of Volkswagen management's multi-brand strategy.

The example of Skoda's brand vision emphasizes that there was nothing inevitable about its derivation from the brand promise and that it was chosen as one of several possible strategic options. Though there is nothing automatic about this process, McKinsey's work with its various clients has shown the value of this simple but very effective format. It forces the brand management to clarify the brand promise, looking at it from the customer's point of view.

Figure 3.17 shows two examples of this type of brand promise. Nivea is often cited as a model of successful brand management, although increasing competitive pressure and price erosion have left their traces. Nivea's brand success is clearly expressed in the promise of its brand. It consistently conveys »personal care,« »gentle care,« and »products for sensitive skin.« Even in its expansion into new product sectors, its products and other tools of the marketing mix remain devoted to the brand promise.

Sixt has developed an innovative image as a car rental service that provides exceptionally good value. In less than two decades, Sixt has grown from being a regional player in the German market into a global car rental company offering services in 75 countries (and the market leader in Germany). In 1987, Sixt's share of the German car rental market was just 5 percent; by 2005, its market share had grown to 26 percent. Between 1995 and 2005, Sixt's total revenue increased from EUR 867 million to EUR 1.34 billion over the course of ten years.[4] At the heart of this success is the brand promise »a lot of car for a little money.« This slogan is always the focus in Sixt's conspicuous advertising campaigns.